When Pop Took Us Fishing

The crew of the Lucky Seven prepare for an afternoon's fishing as they wait for the incoming tide to get them afloat.

Pine Pont 1959

Robert Kingsley Hawes

When Pop Took Us Fishing. Copyright © 2016 Robert Kingsley Hawes.

ISBN 978-0-9925421-9-1

All rights reserved. No part of this publication may be reproduced, stored in any retrieval system, or transmitted in any form or by any means electronic, mechanical, recording or otherwise, without the prior permission of the author.

First published in Australia by Sunshine Press.

Cover design by James Hickey.

Publication production by Connie M. Berg.

For further information, contact the author at r.hawes70@gmail.com.

In memory of my beloved wife, Rosemary Hawes, who said I should write a story for the grandkids.

This is for Thomas, Max, Sophie, and Abbey.

Acknowledgements

This book is the personal recollections of the author, together with information he has researched.

His thanks go out to Pam Harmer and Peter Davey for providing historical information about the Pine Point district and giving access to their personal memorabilia and photos.

He also wishes to thank his brother Frank and sister-in-law Deirdre, for their involvement in the writing of this book.

Finally, he wishes to thank Connie Berg and members of the Paddocks Creative Writing Group, for the role they play in mentoring those who wish to get their story out into the world.

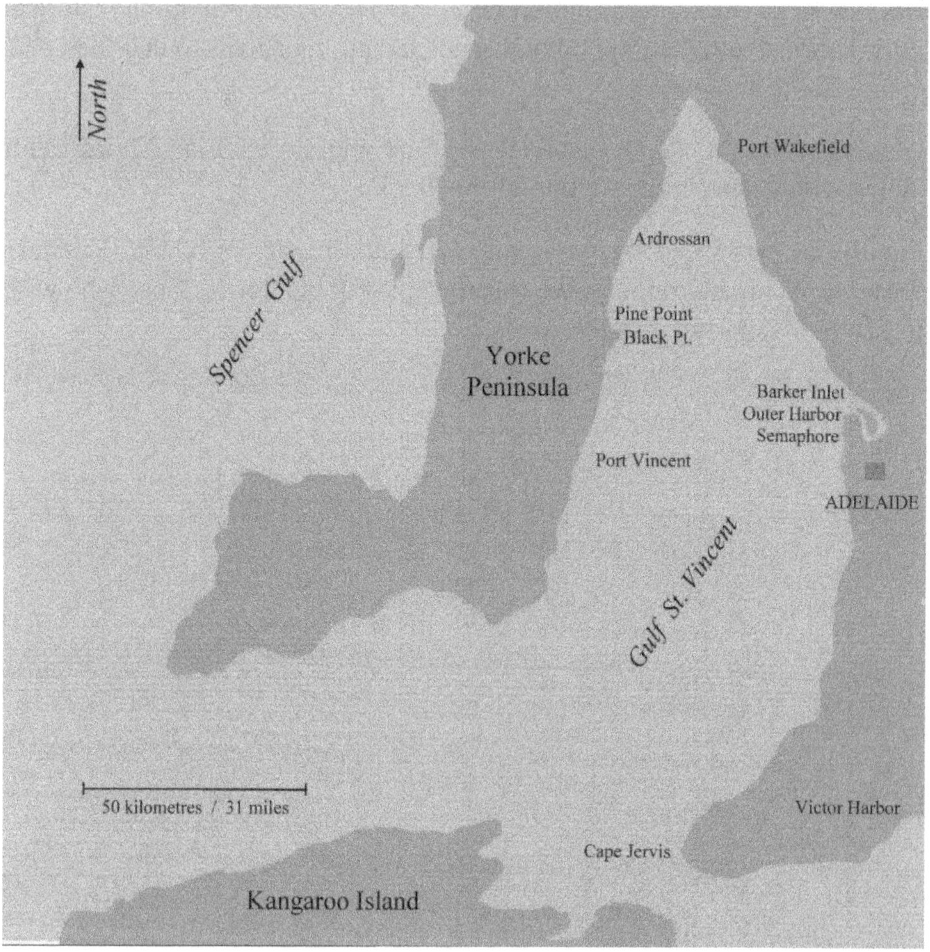
North
Port Wakefield
Ardrossan
Spencer Gulf
Pine Point
Black Pt.
Yorke
Peninsula
Barker Inlet
Outer Harbor
Semaphore
Port Vincent
ADELAIDE
Gulf St. Vincent
50 kilometres / 31 miles
Victor Harbor
Cape Jervis
Kangaroo Island

1 THE OUTDOORS MAN

Most families have interesting stories to tell, and ours is no exception. We were a family of novice fishermen who were among the lucky few to be the first to explore an area of unfished sea. What we saw is no longer there to be seen, and what we did can never be done again. Our story took place at a time when people had very little, but anything was possible.

I was born in 1945, and for me, this is where the story begins. To know the things that drove my Pop, however, I need to go back in time. Pop, or Frank Hawes senior, as most knew him, was born at Warragul, Victoria, in 1905. He was the only child of Fred and Agnes Hawes. Agnes was always affectionately called Matie.

Fred and Matie Hawes' wedding, 1904. From left: Jane (sister), Jack (brother), Matie (Agnes, bride), Jane (mother), Fred (groom), and Nora (sister-in-law). Father of the bride, Charles Manning, is conspicuously missing, but they appear to have left a space for him.

Matie owned a farm in Gippsland, 50 miles east of Warragul. The farm was her dowry.

Her father, Charles Manning, was one of thousands who had sought riches in the Victoria Gold Rush. He and his partner, Patrick Sinnett (or Synett), were among the lucky. They struck gold near Rushworth and called their mine the Crown Cross. The Crown Cross was one of Victoria's most productive gold mines in the 1880s.

Charles Manning gave each of his three children a farm and then disappeared from family history. We believe he was gone by the time Matie married, for the father of the bride is conspicuously absent from her wedding photo.

All we know is that he had a colourful reputation. They called him Champagne Charlie, for he only drank champagne and would shout the bar every night. Pop told this story many times, and I recall once seeing a TV documentary on the Victorian Gold Rush.

"They might say something about Champagne Charlie," Pop remarked as we settled down to watch the show.

We both knew there was little prospect of that, but to Pop's great delight, we were wrong. Great grandpa featured as a gold rush success story. Not only did they call him Champagne Charlie and tell how he shouted the bar, they actually had a sketch of him doing it. Dressed finer than your average gold miner, he was surrounded by ladies, whose attire would have caught the attention of most gentlemen in the bar that night.

"Do you think one of those ladies is my great grandma?" I asked.

"Don't know." Pop's answer sounded rather vague.

Pop was a country boy, though he spent much of his childhood at Melbourne's Wesley College, where he boarded as a student. He hoped to one day be a farmer, but that chance was lost when his parents separated. Matie sold the farm, and Pop was left to make his way in the big city. Matie lived to be almost 100, supported for many years by the proceeds of her dowry. Pop's only benefit from a fortune made from gold was his good education.

Fortunately, city life had its benefits. It provided Pop with endless sporting opportunities, and he was a keen sportsman. On my bookcase, I have a cricket ball presented by the Bentleigh Cricket Club.

Bentleigh
A N A C C
Presented to F Hawes
Bowling Performance
Semi Final 1932-33
10 Wickets for 37 Runs

Pop also played Australian Rules Football, but only kept one memento. The damage gained from an unfortunate ruck duel always showed on his chest x-rays. However, tennis provided Pop with his most cherished prize. It was while playing tennis that he met Mum.

Pop began his career in the office of the British Tobacco Company, while continuing his studies, part time, through the Hemmingway and Robertson Institute. He qualified as an accountant and then went on to earn a Diploma of Commerce at the Melbourne University. Pop had an academic gift and read extensively on philosophy and psychology, but took no formal study in those subjects. He only saw value in qualifications that gave him a good income.

Pop often told of a close shave he had while working for the British Tobacco Company. The year was 1925. Pop was 19, and he had just walked out of the tobacco company's new, four story building, still under construction in Melbourne's Swanston Street. He heard a loud noise, turned, and witnessed the infamous collapse of that building. Four construction workers were killed. Insufficient cement in the concrete was blamed for the failure. Pop had avoided the catastrophe by seconds.

There are many types of luck. Pop had the type that enables a person to walk away, when the outcome should have been much worse. Pop's luck stayed with him always, though he pushed it many times.

In 1929, Pop married Mum. Now 24-years old, his career was flourishing and he was Chief Accountant for the British Tobacco Company. Mum was 20, but the timing was bad. It was the beginning of the Great Depression. They took out a mortgage and purchased Mum's dream house. However, fear of unemployment meant the tobacco company could drive their workers hard. In 1933, exhaustion from long hours of work caused Pop to quit his job. With no income, the family walked out of Mum's dream house. Every penny saved was lost to the bank.

The family moved in with Matie, who had a nice house in the Melbourne seaside suburb of Black Rock. It was the height of the Great Depression, and Pop's ambition to forge a career in commerce had been crushed. He yearned for the country. As a boy, his father had taught him everything he needed to know about the rabbit industry. The fashion for men's hats required a steady flow of rabbit skins. Pop had an idea.

Pop left the family and went north to the Hay Plains, where he joined his father, Fred, in the town of Moulamein. Fred owned a truck and had a contract to carry railway ballast. Pop set himself up as a rabbit skin buyer. Rabbits were thick in the area. The local aboriginal community provided the skins, which Pop on sold to regional skin buyers. Pop had a partner, an aboriginal person called Cooper. Pop entrusted Cooper to do the buying, which meant Cooper held most of the money, and the aboriginal community knew where he kept it. Mum once questioned the security of the arrangement, but Pop assured her that they were fine people who could be trusted, and he was right.

At times, Pop would help his father. Fred was a true bushie, and Pop often told the story of them being camped by a small waterhole. In the water was a dead cow. Ignoring the effect that rotting flesh has on water quality, Fred filled the billy and brewed some tea. Pop questioned what he was being asked to drink. "Boiling kills the germs," was Fred's reply.

Pop took the brew, not wishing to appear weak in the eyes of his father. He sipped slowly, hoping all germs were dead. He survived. The germs must have been dead, but he never forgot the taste. Pop learned two things. Boiling kills germs, and bush living kills taste buds. His father's taste buds were all dead.

By 1936, Fred's trucking business was more than he could handle. Pop gave up skin buying to help his father. Shortly thereafter, the whole family moved to Moulamine. At first, they stayed in the hotel, and later, rented a small house in the town. Mum had her first taste of country living. It lasted two years, and then they all moved back to the city.

On arrival back in Melbourne, Pop considered his options for employment. The British Tobacco Company had killed his ambition to succeed in the corporate world. He sought advice from his former tutors, the Hemingway and Robertson Institute. They specialised in correspondence courses for students unable to attend universities or similar teaching organisations. Their courses enabled their students to become members of professional bodies in fields such as accountancy. Hemingway and Robertson offered Pop a job as one of their salesmen. Pop remained with that organisation for the rest of his working life, during which time he grew a useful network of contacts in both commerce and government.

Pop was an enigma, an outdoorsman with an academic's intellect. Though at times called upon to speak at graduation ceremonies, few who knew him would have guessed that his true passion lay in the great outdoors. I doubt that Mum fully understood his passion when she married him.

Mum was a city girl who somehow married a country boy. Born in 1908, her parents were Walter and Annie Tandy. Mum had two sisters, Emma and Elsie, and a younger brother, Wally. Emma was the oldest, but a burst appendix took her life when she was just 14. Mum always kept Emma's photo on her bedroom mantelpiece.

Mum's family lived on High Street, in the Melbourne suburb of Malvern. Their business made quality furniture, crafted to meet the specific requirements of wealthy Melbourne households. The home, the furniture workshop, and the furniture show room, were all on the one premises. The family enjoyed a good, middle-class, Melbourne lifestyle.

Mum's first and only job was that of bookkeeper for the Dandenong Bacon Factory. The Roaring Twenties was the era of her teens, and she relished the social life of a big city. She envisaged that little of her perfect world would ever change, and that one day she would marry a man who fitted that world. Little did she realise that destiny would see her future husband take her on an adventure far removed from everything that gave her comfort. But Pop chose well, for Mum had the fortitude to meet every challenge.

Mum enjoyed the social life of a big city. This treasured page from her scrap book records an event when as an 18-year-old, she caught the eye of a camera man whilst participating in Melbourne's Henley on the Yarra celebration of 1927.

2 MY FAMILY

In 1945, I had the good fortune to be born at Semaphore, in a small community hospital on the foreshore. Semaphore is part of the Port Adelaide district. Five years earlier, my family had moved from their home in Victoria to begin a new life in South Australia. It turned out that fate had put us in a good spot. Though we did not know it then, the waters of Gulf St. Vincent that shimmered through the hospital windows in the afternoon sun would soon change our lives.

Gulf St. Vincent sits facing the South Pole, tucked midway along the southern coast of the Great Australian Continent. It was one of the last corners of the globe to be reached by seafaring explorers. The first settlers arrived on its shore a mere 109 years before I was born, and from that settlement grew the city of Adelaide. At the time I was born, few people in the city realised that nature had placed a marine jewel on their doorstep.

Fate also saw me born at a good time, for World War II would end in the year of my arrival. New times were coming, and I was there to welcome them. They would begin as gentle times, for everyone was sick of conflict. It was a less competitive world, with people more inclined to help one another. The war had touched all. Those who went away, experienced horrors they could never talk about. Those who stayed behind, had years of worry and hardship. Many lost loved ones, or had them return, broken in spirit and body. When peace came, it was embraced by all, and for years thereafter, there was no need for our local policeman to carry a gun.

Australia is often called the Land of Opportunity, and in the years that followed the war, this was particularly true. Our family was one of many who turned things around in the amazing fifties.

My arrival at Semaphore was not considered a blessing, however, for up until then, my parents' marriage had only seen hard times. Married at the beginning of the Great Depression, by the mid-1930s, they had three small mouths to feed. Ten years later, I arrived as an unplanned number four.

Our family was typical of most at that time. We had no car and went everywhere by foot, bicycle, bus, or train. We knew no one who owned a refrigerator. Things that needed to be kept cool were placed in an ice chest. The ice truck would come down the street on appointed days, and people would run out and buy their ice. Perishable food was mostly eaten on the day of purchase.

Things were scarce after the war, and butter was rationed. Mum kept a careful eye on her butter coupons. Evenings were usually spent listening to the radio, reading, or playing cards.

My sister Gwynne was the oldest. She was born in 1930 and left home to teach in the country when I was four. I was told she studied hard as a student and did well at school, a story most often told when I brought my report card home. Gwynne never returned from the country. No doubt, Pop understood her liking for the place. Gwynne married and settled in the town of Renmark, where she raised four boys and a girl on their family fruit block. Gwynne was a talented artist and enjoyed painting tranquil landscapes of the Murray River.

My sister Gwynne standing alongside one of her paintings.

My eldest brother Frank was born two-years later, in 1932. He was a gifted student, something he inherited from Pop. He earned a full scholarship to St Peters College, Adelaide's most prestigious private school.

Frank continued his scholastic achievements at Saints, with one incident being of particular note. On that occasion, the school sprung a surprise test on all the year-10 students, a little over 100 boys. All were summoned to the school physics lecture room where they were given a formal IQ examination, consisting of a series of tests done against the clock. Its purpose was to establish the IQ rating of each student.

Frank achieved a score of 160, the highest score possible. Pop was told that it was the highest score the school had ever seen. However, some in the school faculty concluded that such a result had to be flawed and initiated an investigation into the reliability of the test. My parents were told that they could tell no one, including Frank, how well he had done. Frank found out 50 years later, when Mum told him. I suspect the exam result was correct, and Pop most likely had a similar gift.

By age 19, Frank was a fully qualified accountant. It took him two years to complete a course that took most of Pop's students an average of seven. Though blessed with an ability, Frank never went to university. Pop thought accountancy provided the best income prospects for a young person starting out, and that is what Frank was encouraged to do. Frank was also an accomplished sportsman and gained selection in the State's Amateur League Football Team.

My brother Lloyd was born in 1936, shortly before the family moved to Moulamine. He was our unlucky brother, born with a disability, which in those days could neither be properly diagnosed or treated. His muscles would spasm, making him restless and sleep difficult. Periods of concentration were hard, and schoolwork or holding down a job were things he was not equipped to handle. Living in a household where his older brother was the yardstick for achievement was not easy. Lloyd left home in his early teens, a note on his bed simply read, *Gone forever.*

Lloyd's life from that point on was one I would love to tell, but alas, he died in a car accident in 1971. He was 35 years old, and I only know scraps of what he did and saw. It was at times when bad health drove him home and Mum would nurse him back to wellness that I would hear of his adventures.

Lloyd spent much of his life on ketches, the large sailing vessels that carried cargo between the many small ports and jetties dotted along South Australia's coastline. The ketches provided essential transport, as country roads at the time were few, and mainly dirt.

At other times, Lloyd would head for the outback, where there were various aboriginal communities and outback cattle stations that always had a welcome for him. On one occasion, the Salvation Army told us they found him living under a tank stand. Lloyd was too proud to be known by his peers as an invalid pensioner, but by age 30, Mum convinced him that he had no other choice.

I was the youngest and did not enjoy school. I hated studying subjects I had no use for, such as Latin. As a sportsman, my achievements fell well short of my eldest brother's. Catching lots of fish off the Semaphore Jetty was the thing I did best, but no one regarded that as a worthy ability.

The family's move from Victoria to South Australia had been full of trepidation. People in Melbourne thought of Adelaide as a small, backward city, where nothing interesting happened. The family had no friends or relatives in Adelaide and knew very little about the place. They had always considered Melbourne to be their home and were happy to live there. But Hemmingway and Robertson had offered Pop a transfer, where he would be the boss. The offer was too good to refuse. In 1940, the family arrived in Adelaide with very little other than Pop's new job.

Among Pop's personal papers, I found this cutting attached to a letter sent to him by his cousin, Allie Ford, in 1980. I do not know where she found the cutting, but it was something she must have kept in her possession for forty years.

At first, they rented in Adelaide's more affluent eastern suburbs, but soon realised rents were more affordable in the Port Adelaide district. There was a good reason for this, for Port Adelaide was considered a working man's suburb, not the address you associate with well-to-do people.

Port Adelaide, for those who lived there, was a great place. There were the beaches, the jetties, speedboats at Snowden's Beach, and the Semaphore Side Shows, with open-air concerts every night throughout summer. You could swim, fish, sail, or play football. If you lived in Port Adelaide and someone tried to put you down, you reminded them that your district had a football team that had won more premierships than any other. In those days, the Port Adelaide team drew its talent locally, and the players played with a determination to make their district proud. Pop, being a typical Victorian, loved Australian Rules Football, and Port Adelaide was Football Heaven. He quickly became a staunch, one-eyed, Port Adelaide supporter.

Lloyd loved the Port also. He knew of no other place where there was a pub on every corner. "Wear your welcome out in one," he once explained, "and you just move on to the next."

Lloyd loved the ketches, the fishing boats, and the people of the Port. Port Adelaide bustled in those days. The wharfs were the centre of activity. Unlike today's empty waterfront, wharf-space was at a premium. Shipping filled the docks. The commercial fishing boats were crammed next to the Jervois Bridge, and the large fleet of coastal trading ketches docked wherever the big ships left room. Sometimes, ketches would be three-abreast at the wharf. Lloyd always found work on the ketches, though mostly unpaid, for he could not do the labouring. He would earn his voyage as helmsman. He loved being at sea.

3   THE STORY BEGINS

Pop tried hard to make a new home in Adelaide, a city Melbourne people considered little more than a big country town. However, the smaller city actually suited Pop, though a country town would have suited him even more. Even a small city made him restless. Each day he would go to work in his dull city office, for that was the path his education had put him on. He was State Principal for the Hemmingway and Robertson Institute. On weekends, he gardened or went to the football, but he wanted something more. He considered fishing, for the Semaphore Jetty was close to home.

Pop had never shown much interest in fishing. Mum said they once fished on Melbourne's Port Philip Bay, and she caught a Flathead. Frank only had the one memory. It related to the time the family returned from Moulamine. Pop set up springers to catch Murray Cod in the Murrumbidgee River. Springers were made from branches chopped from trees, which fishermen set up along the river bank. They acted as fixed fishing poles that reached out over the water. From each springer, a baited hook dangled into the river, attached by a short length of line. Overnight, the fish would come along and catch themselves.

Over several nights, Pop amassed a catch of 23 cod. He only kept fish that exactly fitted a banana crate and rejected any that were too big or too small. To keep the fish alive, he fastened line through their noses and tethered them in the water. Tethering was a common practice in those days, and no one thought it cruel. On the day of departure, Pop packed his fish in a banana crate and used grape leaves and wet hessian to keep them cool. The crate travelled to Melbourne strapped to the back of Pop's T Model Ford, and the fish were sold on arrival.

Pop had never fished off a jetty and wondered what the Semaphore Jetty had to offer. Our family odyssey began the day Pop took a walk along the Semaphore Jetty. There, he discovered a group of fishermen catching Tommy Ruffs. Tommies were not known to

Pop, as they are uncommon in Victoria. He asked a few questions, taking careful note of the gear and bait being used. Then he went home, and over the next few days, assembled what was needed.

Ben Jameson's hardware shop on Semaphore Road had all his tackle requirements. First, there was the fishing rod. For this, he purchased a 13-foot Indian cane, together with some porcelain runners, and cord to bind them to the rod. Next, he purchased a four-inch, centre-pin, Bakelite reel, and a spool of recently invented, nylon fishing line. For his creel, he found a wooden box of suitable size and shape. He partitioned the box into two compartments, one side for gear and bait, the other for the catch. Always the optimist, the catch side was the larger of the two. Then he attached a carrying strap, and finally a lid, for he did not want his catch jumping out.

The only thing remaining was the bait, and this was something he had to explain to Mum in a gentle, but persuasive manner. Gents were the requirement, generally referred to by non-fisher-folk as maggots. They were cheap; in fact, you bred them yourself in the back yard. The only problem you might face is having to explain a smell to the neighbours. Leave a few fish scraps out to be flyblown, wrap them in newspaper, then bury them in the garden. A few days later, you dig them up, your wriggling harvest ready to be put into nice fresh bran. Simple, and if you dug them up on a windy day, the smell would go right down the street, and no one would figure out where it was coming from.

Storage was the other issue. They needed a cool place, and the coolest place was in the ice chest, alongside the food. They would be in a glass jar with a lid, from which no maggot in the history of maggots, had ever been known to escape. Pop was a good salesman. He secured the necessary permission and began the breeding of his bait.

On suitable evenings, Pop would hop on his bike and head for the Semaphore Jetty. Tommies on toast became a family favourite and still are to this day. Mum would prepare several slices of toast, smother them in butter, and then cut the slices into quarters. At the same time, she would fry a batch of Tommy fillets. Next, she would pile toast and Tommies onto two separate plates, from which you helped yourself. You took a Tommy fillet, peeled away the skin, scraped off the dark flesh, put the white flesh on a quarter of toast, sprinkled a good quantity of salt, and yum. It was a messy way to eat a fish, but freshly caught Tommies have a unique sweetness that makes the whole process worthwhile.

Pop's Tommy fishing skills developed quickly, and soon all the neighbours were eating Tommy Ruffs. This was a good thing, for it made them more forgiving of the occasional stench coming from the backyard. When Pop ran out of hungry neighbours, he set up a smoke box and smoked his surplus catch. Fish quickly spoiled in an ice chest, but smoked fish remained tasty for several days.

4 THE PRAM

In 1947, Pop's fishing moved to the next phase. Often, he would notice a rowboat on the blue-line, a short distance out from the Semaphore Jetty. For those unfamiliar with the term blue-line, it is the line where the pale green water of the sandy shallows meets the deep blue water further out. A blue line runs the full length of the Adelaide metropolitan coast.

The rowboat aroused Pop's curiosity, so one day he waited for it to come in. He asked the boatie if he had had any luck and was shown a catch of King George Whiting. King George Whiting is a fish renowned for its texture and fine flavour. Averaging a little under a pound in weight, most people considered them a luxury, their price more than they could afford.

"Only those who can afford to pay, know the luxury of eating King George Whiting," was how Pop successfully promoted the idea of buying a rowboat to Mum.

Shortly thereafter, Pop was owner of his first boat, a 10-foot, blunt nosed, bondwood and canvas dinghy, commonly known as a pram. Pop's pram was a Navy disposal item, built to withstand the rigors of World War II. Appropriately painted battle ship grey, it sat on a wooden trailer that relied on bicycle wheels for mobility. The boat and trailer were light enough to be pushed to the beach on foot. Pop was proud of his new boat, and would feel a little indignant when other fishermen called it the butter box.

From that point on, Pop would learn everything the hard way. His first boating misadventure occurred on a day that my sister Gwynne was drafted to be his crewman. Gwynne remembers the day well. She was 18 at the time. The departure was uneventful, their destination, the Whiting holes just out from the jetty. The weather looked a little dodgy, but Pop was not going to let one black cloud stop a good day's fishing. Gwynne had reservations. The black cloud made her feel uneasy, and Pop's assurances that if worst came to worst, they were within swimming distance of shore, did little to help.

History tells that they should have stayed home that day, for the black cloud edged closer, then without warning, unleashed a mighty wind that unroofed houses on the foreshore and blew trees out of the ground. The sea turned to rolling mountains, and the tops of the waves were whipped into the air, creating blizzard like conditions that surrounded the little boat. Gwynne remembers the quick weighing of the anchor, then surfing in on what appeared to her to be just the one wave. She remembers the boat being dumped on top of seaweed. The journey from start to finish had been frightening, but quick. That was the day Gwynne formed great admiration for Pop's seamanship, but a poor opinion on his reading of the weather. That was also the day Pop first did battle with what was to become his nemesis - *The Curse of the Westerly Wind*.

Pop's luck had served him well that day, but the experience taught him nothing. All it did was give him a belief that he could handle anything the sea could throw at him. It was no surprise therefore, that Frank soon had his own harrowing story to tell.

Frank regularly fished with Pop in that rather cramped little boat, but it was not falling overboard or capsizing that eventually got them into trouble, it was curiosity about what other much bigger boats were doing. These boats would often motor past as they voyaged to a fishing ground further out. Pop was told by local grocer and keen fisherman, Norrie Rix, that these boats were after Snapper on the Norma wreck, some three miles offshore. This was exciting news, for Pop had long carried the ambition to one day catch a big Snapper. Snapper grew to 35 pounds in weight, and were highly prized as eating fish. Those boats were after Snapper, and he could join them with fewer than 5,000 strokes of the oars. I doubt if many have ever ventured to the Norma wreck in a ten-foot rowboat, but in 1948, Pop and Frank did it a number of times.

It was the final row in from the Norma that Frank remembers so well. He was 16 at the time. It was the first calm day after several days of rough weather. They arrived on the Norma mid-morning and fished until mid-day, by which time the sea breeze began to stir. This was the signal to up-anchor and get in before the sea became too rough. They had just passed the Wonga Shoal light, the halfway point to land, when Pop noticed something unusual.

Frank was on the stern seat looking forward. Pop was rowing, looking back over Frank's shoulder. The water was cloudy, due to the previous few days of rough weather. Pop's gaze was set on the horizon, until a large mass of submerged seaweed caught his eye. It was just behind Frank, but somehow, it was staying with the boat. Pop wondered how this was, but each time he thought he might get a better look, it would sink from view. Finally, it established itself about four feet behind and just below the surface. Pop confirmed his suspicion. It was not seaweed.

"What's that?" he asked Frank. It was an odd question, for Pop already knew the answer. Frank turned to see what he later described as a large, grey cone, in the water just behind him. His reaction was almost as odd as Pop's question. He got off his seat and hid on the floor of the boat.

The pram's transom was about three feet wide, and Frank estimated the shape in the water to be about the same width. It stayed with them, maintaining distance and depth. It was a massive head, featureless, except for two small black eyes that appeared to be focused on Frank.

Frank peeped over the transom, staring into the eyes, one at a time. The head was so close and the eyes so far apart, that one eye at a time was the best he could manage. Beyond the head, he could see a giant pair of pectoral fins, spread like wings, but everything else was hidden in the murky water. The creature was huge.

This head-on view of a monster White Pointer shark from such an insecure vantage point, has stayed with Frank all his life. It followed them, as if trying to decide what benefit there was in attacking this little boat. A 10-foot boat was no match for an 18-foot shark, but the shark appeared uncertain about that.

Pop rowed on with careful oar stokes, thinking any careless splashing of the blades might excite the unwelcomed visitor into unthinkable action. The situation remained unchanged for about 15 minutes, at which point the shark lost interest and swam away.

This was their first encounter with a big shark. It left them wondering how common these creatures were, and how big did they grow. They had no way of knowing that they would soon be learning a lot about big sharks.

5 TROUBLE ON THE WATER

The White Pointer incident convinced Pop to buy a small outboard motor, so that he could outrun the sharks. That at least was the theory, for the fact was, he had no idea how fast they could swim.

The new motor was shiny silver, with a promising brand name, Speed. From its first outing, this motor earned a place in family folk lore. It relished the open sea. The return to land was the problem. At the beach, it would start first pull of the cord and quickly have them on their way. Coming home was a different story. It would never start. If it had its way, it would have stayed at sea forever. The Speed outboard earned a new name for itself, The Spud.

For homeward voyages, the pram was once again a rowboat, only now it had a shiny but useless weight hanging off the back. If rowing was to be avoided, Pop had to make sure they were not the last to leave a ground. This way, they could sometimes enlist a tow. Our grocer, Norrie Rix, was one who often towed them in. Norrie was destined to have his own fishing misadventure some years later, but I will tell the story now.

Norrie had a boat, which Pop could only envy, a 15-foot, clinker trailer boat with a Stewart Turner inboard motor. Norrie usually fished at the Malcolm, a ground that in later times became known as the Semaphore Reef. On Norrie's day of trouble, the fish were biting so well on the Malcolm, that neither he nor his mate Jacko, nor brother-in-law Jim Hay, took notice of a ketch in the distance. It was the *Coringle*, steering its usual erratic course as it headed for Outer Harbor. The *Coringle* had a mismatch of power between its two propellers and was notorious for being impossible to steer in a straight line. Eventually, Norrie did notice the ketch, for it appeared to be heading in their direction.

"Cheeky blighters," Norrie commented. "They obviously want to see what we're catching."

They went on fishing. When next they looked up, the ketch was very close indeed and was now heading directly for them. They stopped fishing and watched the bow loom closer and closer, until the bow was all they could see. The wheelhouse was obscured, which meant the helmsman could not see them.

"They don't know we're here," Norrie yelled.

There was panic on Norrie's boat. One went for the anchor, while Norrie grabbed the starter handle on the motor. He gave the handle its hardest crank ever. The Stewart Turner engine was considered the Rolls Royce of boat engines at the time. Unlike most engines, where you either grabbed the flywheel or used a strap to start the motor, the Stewart Turner had a sophisticated starter handle, attached to the flywheel by a chain.

Norrie's mighty crank on the starter handle somehow snapped the chain. Sometimes, it pays not to go that little extra in an emergency. The men looked at each other with that *what do we do now look.* What happened next, made sad reading for Pop when he read his paper the next day. *What a tragic loss,* he thought. *That wonderful boat, at the bottom of the sea.*

In those days, your local grocer made home deliveries, as few people owned a motor vehicle. When Norrie dropped the groceries in the following Wednesday, he gave Mum the full story, though some was still a blur to him.

He recalled the crash as the ketch hit them amidships. Next, he recalled how cold the water was, and then seeing the bow of his boat pointed skyward, bobbing in the water. He recalled them clinging to the bow, securing grips on the bow stem and capstan. The boat had no floatation. The only thing stopping it from sinking was air trapped under the front deck. At first, they felt they could hang on all day, but that was before they heard the unmistakable hiss of air.

The bow sank lower and lower. Finally, Norrie's left foot made one last contact with his beloved boat, as it sank beneath them, headed for Davey Jones' Locker. They were swimming once again, this time making for the engine box floating nearby. It was the only part of Norrie's boat left floating. It was not very buoyant, but the newspaper said that it saved their lives.

Meanwhile, back on the *Coringle*, crewmembers were looking around, wondering what the loud thump was. All had been below deck, the boat on automatic pilot. Fortunately, one looked over the stern and noticed a white hat in the water. On closer inspection, he realised that it was sitting on someone's head, and that someone had two companions swimming with him. The *Coringle* turned back and made a less than perfect rescue. With the sea running high, it took almost an hour for the awkward steering *Coringle* to manoeuvre into a position where it could pick up its casualties.

6 THE GAMBLER

Snapper fishing created an unexpected problem for Pop. A good catch of 15-pound Snapper was more than the neighbours could handle. What to do with the surplus? Con Scounos' fish shop on Semaphore Road came to the rescue.

In today's world, we are controlled by a bureaucracy. Rules and regulations place barriers on almost every aspect of daily living. Few barriers existed when Pop and Frank caught their first Snapper. Post World War II was a wonderful period of opportunity, where people pursued their ideas without worry of red tape. You could catch as many fish as you wanted and sell them to whomever you wanted. There were few regulations, and the sea had an endless supply of fish. At least, that is what people thought.

Pop sold the surplus fish. Deliveries to Con's shop were made on pushbike, one or two fish at a time. All the while, Pop and Frank were learning more about the Snapper. They discovered night fishing was far more productive than day. They identified lights on the land that they could line up to locate the Norma wreck after dark. Their catches increased to more than the pram could carry. By late 1949, they needed a bigger boat and turned to the newspaper classifieds. They found a 12-foot, bondwood boat for sale. It was not as sturdy as the pram, but weighed about the same. Weight was important, for they had to push it to the beach on the pram's old trailer. Pop bought the bondwood boat, but soon found himself having to make a much bigger purchase.

In January of 1950, a house came on the market. It was in Largs Bay, close to where we rented. It was a house Mum often went out of her way to admire. It was her new dream house. For the past 17 years, we had rented. It had been 14 years since we last owned a motor car. All Mum had to show for 20 years of marriage was four kids. Nothing had turned out the way she expected when she married that promising young business executive in 1929.

However, hard times were not the only reason for Mum's situation. Pop had a vice. He did not drink, and he did not smoke, but racehorses were his downfall. He had a vast knowledge on the subject, and frequently invested on the outcome of horse races. Unfortunately, Pop's luck was seldom with him when he wagered, and his SP bookmaker was often the benefactor of his poor judgement. Mum hated gambling.

As always happens with a dream house, the price was far beyond what my parents could afford. It was a large house, situated on land that went through to the next street. Its exterior had been remodelled, the work of a previous owner, who was an architect. It was a house that caught the eye of many.

In 1950, Mum got her dream house. It had impressive pillars and wide balustrade verandas; the proud creation of a previous owner who was believed to have been an architect. All Pop had to do was work out how he was going to pay the mortgage.

Wide verandas with glazed brick balustrades ran across the front and down one side. Massive pillars supported an expansive roof, and behind the verandas stood walls of solid blue stone. The architect's creation completely captured Mum's imagination.

Pop had already seen Mum's first dream house lost in the Great Depression, and he had always felt responsible. This was his chance to make it up. It was now or never. If he let the opportunity go, another may never come along. The house was purchased. Pop was pushing towards 50. He had 20 years to pay off a big mortgage. When the family lost their first house 17 years earlier, they were left with nothing. They still virtually had nothing, but Pop had a plan to change all that.

Pop began by limiting his gambling investments. This was a good start, but the mortgage still consumed much of what he earned as salary. The house had to contribute. It had two kitchens, two bathrooms, and two laundries. Pop blocked a door in the hallway, turning part of the living area into a self-contained flat. Tenants were taken in. Next, he partitioned the large backyard with fences. One section became Pop's mini poultry farm with 160 chooks, and he sold the eggs. In another area, Pop set up a large vegetable garden. Finally, he planted citrus trees wherever there was room. The 26 almond trees already growing on the property were harvested, and the almonds sold.

However, Pop's plan required one more thing in order to make it work. He had to catch and sell as many Snapper as he could. Hopefully, he would catch enough. As always, he was gambling, but this time he had Mum's approval. She was right behind him.

7 A HOPEFUL START

Everyone was keen to see Pop's plan work. First, Pop established the garden and poultry farm, and then began the task of painting. Frank constructed a floor over the stairwell to the cellar, and incorporated a trapdoor so that we could still get to the stairs. Next, he lined the galvanised iron enclosure that protected the back veranda. These two projects gave the house an extra room.

It was a very busy time for everyone, but time was also needed for fishing. It was an essential part of the plan, and was the element on which Pop had gambled. As it turned out, the gamble was soon looking like a winner. Within months of buying the house, the bondwood boat and trailer could no longer carry home the weight of fish they were catching. Night fishing had proved to be better than expected. Pop had to find another way of doing things. What he required, was a boat he could leave in the water. The mooring would have to be near public transport, which they would use to get to the boat and bring home the fish.

Finding a boat was difficult. There were boats that met the criteria, but none Pop could afford. The house had used up all the spare cash. Finally, Pop found a 12-foot, carvel planked dinghy, moored at the top end of the Port Canal. To be more precise, it had sunk there, but was still attached to the mooring. It had been in that sorry state for some time, which was why he could afford it.

Arrangements were made for salvage, and the boat was brought home, where Frank replaced a number of planks and ribs. Then, he fitted a new, 2.5-horsepower, Chapman Pup, 2-stroke motor. Mum always claimed the credit for Frank's handyman skills. Her family were furniture makers. Pop could not drive a nail, but he was an enthusiastic gardener and painter

Once Frank's work was done, the dinghy went back to its mooring. The mooring was in a good spot, close to the Port Adelaide train station and near a bus stop. This information might puzzle those who know the train station today, for there is no longer a canal. To moor the dinghy there now, would see it sitting in the K-Mart car park.

The new plan worked well. They would catch the bus to the boat and bring the fish home the same way. It is hard to imagine in today's times, two smelly fishermen sitting in a bus, with several sugar bags of large Snapper stacked in the section intended for prams. In 1950, no one thought anything of it.

Frank tells a story, how once they were running to catch the bus, when a hook dangling from his fishing gear went deep into his leg. The bus held back, making sure they would catch it. Once on board, the conductor inspected the imbedded hook, then with true battlefield resolve, said, "Don't worry son, I'll fix that for you in no time."

With that, he pulled out a pocketknife, sterilized the blade with his cigarette lighter, and successfully cut out the hook. Then, he used Frank's handkerchief to bandage the wound. Attitudes shaped by war prevailed in those times.

The mooring's location had one problem. It was at the very top of the Port River. It took one and a half hours to get from the mooring to the river mouth, and a further hour to get to the Norma. They wondered if it were possible to catch Snapper that were closer. Pop sought advice from Norrie Rix, who suggested Pop try at the river mouth. It proved to be a very useful suggestion.

The Port River estuary system has two openings, separated by Torrens Island. Torrens Island is about three square miles in area and is protected by mangrove bushes on all sides. The main river opening is to the south of the island, and is flanked by breakwaters that protect the Outer Harbor wharves. The northern opening, known as the Barker Inlet, is much shallower. They found Snapper at both openings, and these places had a bonus. They were protected and could be fished in almost any weather.

The Barker Inlet proved to be the more productive of the two openings. Frank recalls the evening rush, when a huge school of Snapper would sweep past the boat on sunset, causing the water to turn pink. These fish were headed for feeding grounds further into the inlet.

The discovery of so many Snapper in protected water, changed everything. Bad weather was no longer a problem. They could fish whenever they found the time, and their catches grew in both size and number.

A lot had happened in three years. Pop had owned three boats that had all paid for themselves, and we were now living in a big house, though it was mostly owned by the bank. But Pop's fishing was helping to buy the big house, and he was finding more fish everywhere he looked.

Pop was no doubt wondering why it had taken him almost 50 years to discover fishing, and I think this was when he first began to ponder on the potential of his newfound pastime.

8 THE MAD MAN OF OUTER HARBOR

Pop had a favourite saying; *Nothing worthwhile ever comes easy*. He soon found that the fish around Outer Harbor did not come easy. There was a reason why so few fished there at night. Pop and Frank soon found themselves crossing swords with Outer Harbor's mad man; an eccentric professional fisherman who for many years had regarded the entire gulf as his personal domain.

The mad man's name was Robbie Osborne. Robbie was a mysterious character who lived a reclusive life in a caravan, not far from the Outer Harbor wharf. Most of Port Adelaide's commercial fishermen were based at the Jervois Bridge and fished along the gulf's eastern shore, or ventured south as far as Kangaroo Island. No one knew where Robbie often went, but he always returned with a boatload of Snapper. He was highly respected for his fishing knowledge, but his mad man reputation kept most away. Pop and Frank found themselves encroaching on part of Robbie's mystery territory. The mouth of the Port River estuary system was where Robbie sometimes fished mid-winter.

Robbie owned two boats. His big boat was the Ena. Pop considered the Ena to be the perfect boat for a Snapper fisherman. It was a 26-foot, single masted cutter, capable of staying at sea for several days. In its centre was a large well, which fishing boats of the era often had. Wells were watertight box compartments, sealed against the inside of the hull. Holes through the hull allowed fresh seawater into the well, allowing the catch to be kept alive until returning to port. The Ena's well held a lot of Snapper. Robbie's other boat was a 16-foot open dinghy, which had a large net on the back.

Frank recalls one afternoon when they were trolling for Snook, killing time as they waited for the sun to go down. The Snapper patch was nearby. Robbie was trolling also. Suddenly, they looked around to see the Ena almost on top of them. The two boats turned level, and then Robbie began a now familiar rant.

On the previous few nights, they had all fished the same spot, and Robbie's tirade suggested he was a little resentful. He did not like part-time amateur fishermen moving in on his grounds, stealing the bread from his mouth. He was a professional, and they had other jobs to go to. He went on to emphasise his disapproval by letting them know that if they went anywhere near his ground that night, he had a .303 rifle waiting for them.

Stories of Robbie and his .303 were well known, as were stories that he would happily ram any boat that got in his way. It was said that he had a metal plate in his head, the result of a fall when he was a jockey. Pop was told that Robbie had been a promising steeplechase jockey, but the accident cut short his career. Now he was a fisherman of erratic behaviour. I believe it was a well-known Outer Harbor fishing identity, Tommy Grace, who warned Pop to stay away from Robbie.

Pop had to consider what to do. At stake were the fish they expected to catch that night, against which was a threat of unknown substance. To date, they had fished the Norma in a 10-foot rowboat, been hassled by a White Pointer shark, and Pop had battled the westerly wind. They had no way of knowing how much of the Robbie legend was true. Pop decided to call the mad man's bluff.

An interesting night followed, but apart from repeated tirades of abuse, nothing hostile happened. The infamous .303 rifle stayed out of sight. It was the same whenever they came together after that. The night would begin with Robbie expressing great displeasure and threatening drastic action. Frank would retaliate by telling Robbie where to go, and Pop would ignore all. Pop just kept on fishing. Often, Frank told me stories about the mad man, and as a five-year-old, I imagined him to be the most terrifying person on Earth.

9 THE TEAL

Robbie held one advantage in their psychological war. Snapper fishing at Outer Harbor peaked mid-winter, and the nights were cold. The small dinghy offered little protection from the elements, and its crew was often soaked from the spray that came over the bow. Once the sun was gone, the lightest of breezes would chill their skin as it pierced their sodden clothes. Fortunately, the Snapper soon took their minds off their discomfort. The frantic activity kept them warm.

A few yards away, Robbie fished in luxury, wearing clothes that were warm and dry. The superstructure of the Ena sheltered him from the chilling wind. Robbie enjoyed this advantage, and when the fishing action slowed, he made the most of it. The crew of the dinghy would feel the chill return and looked to their plum jam sandwiches for comfort. Robbie would go below and cook his tea. Pop and Frank had no idea what it was that Robbie cooked, but it smelt delicious. On windy nights, they suspected he threw in extra onions, making sure the smell would not be lost in the breeze.

It was little wonder, therefore, that both Pop and Frank had the same thought when they noticed a for sale sign displayed on an 18-foot launch. The launch had a fully enclosed cabin and a mast, though the mast served no real purpose, for there were no sails. Brass lettering on the bow spelt out the name, *Teal*. It was moored not far from the dinghy.

Next day, the whole family gathered at the Port Canal to inspect the *Teal*. I was impressed by its brass steering wheel, a miniaturised version of what was to be found on a big ship. The fishermen were impressed by the comfort, and Mum was impressed by the fact that it was floating. Mum considered floating to be important. She was surprised that Pop had ignored this basic requirement when purchasing his last boat. She knew they could not expect the same discount, but the fishing was returning a good profit. They found the money and the *Teal* became Pop's fourth boat in as many years.

It gave Pop and Frank great pleasure, that first night, when they proudly positioned the *Teal* alongside the Ena. They were in dry clothes, just like Robbie, and their cabin sheltered them from the wind, just like Robbie's. When Robbie went down to cook his tea, they stretched out in their cabin. They still only had sandwiches, but the smell from Robbie's galley scarcely penetrated their cabin walls.

It did not take long for Pop to realise that the *Teal* came with another benefit. She was far more robust than the dinghy and could be moored in less sheltered water. Pop shifted her mooring to the Outer Harbor mooring basin, close to the river mouth. This saved the long journey along the Port River and public transport was still available, as the Outer Harbor train stopped close to home. This meant they could stay out all night, catching a second lot of fish at dawn, and still be home in time for Frank to go to work.

Work was an issue for Frank, as he had to be on time each morning. Frank had a full time office job, played football, helped renovate the house, and fished whenever Pop required. At times, he regretted not going to university like most of his friends, for he had found the study of accountancy to be dull and lacking in challenge. In later life, he discovered that success does not require a university degree.

Compared to Frank, Pop had few time constraints, for he was the boss of where he worked. His job came with flexible hours, and he could spend the first part of the day selling fish and talk to students in the evening.

The *Teal* proved to be a good investment, and on a calm night in the spring of 1950, she proved her worth in another way. They were fishing the Norma, for the seasonal run at Outer Harbor had finished. Suddenly, they came under attack by bandits. Every time they had a Snapper, a shark would rip it off their line. Pop almost landed one fish, when a 10-foot shark grabbed it. For an encore, the shark slammed the side of the boat. Not to be beaten, Pop started to haul in another, this time almost getting it into the boat. A shark bit it in half. Pop kept pulling and lifted the head out of the water, but the shark had not given up. It leapt out of the water and grabbed the head. This time, the encore included a splashing of the *Teal*'s crew. It was a smaller shark than the first, proving several sharks were in the action.

The night's fishing was ruined. It was their first experience with Bronze Whaler sharks, also known as South Australian Whalers. They headed home, cursing their luck, but thankful the event had not happened two years earlier, when they would have been in the pram. The pram might not have handled the encores that went with the shark's performance.

The *Teal*'s size may have saved them from that disaster, but the boat had one failing, not anticipated. It did not handle well in heavy seas. At times, you could spin that rather impressive steering wheel, and it was as if you had done nothing at all. This was the case a few months later, when Pop had his second encounter with *The Curse of the Westerly Wind*. As before, his predicament was due to his indifference to threatening weather. His new boat made him feel invincible.

Pop and Frank were fishing off Outer Harbor when the westerly struck. They found themselves trapped. The seas were too heavy for going south and entering the Port River through the breakwaters. Heading north to the Barker Inlet was also not an option. The only way home was to run with the waves, due east, and go over the Section Bank that separated the final stretch of the Port River from the open sea.

They had never gone that way before, for most times the bank was either too shallow, or dry. Not a problem this day, for the wind pushed the tide up much higher than usual. The *Teal* surfed over the bank with ease, and then Pop spun the wheel to starboard. The intended course was the nearby Outer Harbor mooring basin. This manoeuvre would have put the *Teal* beam on to the waves, but Pop was confident his vessel could handle it. However, the *Teal* had other ideas and ignored the instruction from the helm. It surfed on, crossing the Port River, crossing the tidal flat on the other side, and finishing up in the mangroves. There it stayed for two weeks, waiting for a tide high enough to re-float it. Even when that tide came, we had to dig a channel, for what had stranded the *Teal* was a storm surge much higher than a normal tide.

10 THE JALOPY

For almost two years, Pop explored the waters off Outer Harbor. Then in late 1952, Outer Harbor became just another phase in Pop's fishing story. Pop's story could be summarised as a series of phases, each ended by a problem. He could have stopped at any time and settled for what he was doing, but he was never satisfied. Each time, he would find a solution to the problem and move to a new phase. With each new phase came more fish. The problem that arose in the Outer Harbor phase was too many fish. Pop was catching more Snapper that Con Scounos could sell in his shop. Pop had to find other outlets, but to reach them he needed a motor vehicle.

At the time, a motor vehicle was something Pop could not afford. Frank looked around to see if he could find anything with wheels that would do the job. However, the second-hand car market was sparse in the years following the war. After much searching, Frank found a 1923, Kangaroo Model Chevrolet. If available today, that old bomb would be a high priced, rare, vintage motor vehicle. In 1951, it sold as a bomb, battling to stay out of the junk yard. They christened it the Jalopy.

The Jalopy had a cabin with a single seat. At the back was a wooden buckboard tray. A high metal roof covered the tray, and from it hung fabric side curtains. To start the engine, you turned a crank handle at the front. The jalopy was incapable of speed, a good thing, for it handled like a blancmange on wheels.

The old girl had led a long, hard, life, but Frank thought he could squeeze one last deed out of her. Little did we realise, what a heroic deed it would be. The Jalopy was the catalyst that pushed Pop's fishing to a new frontier. She served her main purpose well, and transported the catch to market for more than a year. However, Pop then realised that she could provide a secondary benefit, and this benefit ultimately had the greatest impact. The Jalopy enabled ice to be carried to the *Teal*, and with ice came the ability to stay out more than one day. The Jalopy gave Pop what he needed to begin his exploration of the gulf.

11 THE WESTERN SHORE

The spring of 1952 saw Pop begin his exploration. It was a big step, for Pop had no idea what was out there. Lloyd knew the gulf well, because the ketches on which he sailed plied its many trade routes. However, Lloyd was away on one of his many walkabouts in 1952. Pop doubted if Lloyd could suggest where to look, anyway. Lloyd had never mentioned places where he had seen people fishing. Pop asked Norrie Rix where he should go. Norrie told him about the Orontes Bank, where large quantities of Snapper were taken during the summer months. This was of interest to Pop, because his Snapper fishing went off in summer.

The Orontes was due west of Outer Harbor, and a few miles out from Port Vincent, a town on the other side of the gulf. The Orontes was the domain of the fishermen living in that town. Pop had to find it.

The plan was simple. Set off from Outer Harbor at nightfall and motor west all night. By dawn, they would be approaching the Orontes, seaward of any Port Vincent boat that might be fishing at the time. They would have the sun behind them, making it possible to line up marks on other boats before being noticed.

Unfortunately, simple plans do not always work out, for the first boat they saw was moored at Port Vincent. They passed it mid-morning, as they motored into the Port Vincent wharf. They spent the day on land, gathering information.

They discovered Port Vincent to be a pretty town, sitting on the shore of a picturesque bay. The town provided the surrounding farms with a complete range of services. It had an unspoiled remoteness about it. Not many tourists ever drove the 60 miles of dirt road to get there.

The bay, which was responsible for the town's location, was rimmed by a beach of clean white sand, and the water close to shore was of good depth. A sandbar, in the form of a spit, ran diagonally out to sea from the bay's southern point. They estimated the spit to be about a mile long. It gave good protection to the boats moored in the bay.

They asked the locals about the fishing, but the fisherman's code of silence held strong. Pop would have to find out for himself, and this would take time. How to do this? It had taken all night just to get there. It would take several trips to check the place out. The journey by sea took too long. They had to come by road, leaving their boats moored at Port Vincent. For this to happen, they first needed to find a suitable place for a base.

The beach adjacent to the town cemetery met all requirements. It was accessible via the cemetery road and far enough from town to be out of everybody's way. Add to this, the water there was protected by the spit, making it ideal for mooring the *Teal* and dinghy. Finding a site for a base was a good start, but they still had a problem. The Jalopy was not capable of making the 300-mile round trip.

They sailed back to Outer Harbor and in the following days, again tackled the sparse second-hand car market. They had to upgrade the Jalopy, but as before, they found nothing they could afford. In desperation, Frank bought a 1937, Austin A7. It was not what they wanted, but with a bit of luck, might do the 300-mile round trip. The Austin had both front and back seats, but no boot. Instead, it had a pull down luggage rack attached at the rear. It was a poor substitute for the buckboard on the Jalopy. To make do, they strapped an old ice chest to the luggage rack. This is how they would carry their fish and ice. The car was a rust bucket.

A memorable feature of the Austin was the front left hand headlight, which stayed attached to the mudguard more courtesy of the electrical wiring, than any remaining metal. This light would swivel to a 45-degree angle. When driving at night, one headlight would shine dimly down the road, the other over the paddocks. People probably assumed they were spotlighting rabbits, but never once did a police patrol pull them over, though that was possibly because they never came across a police patrol.

On the weekend of the big move, Frank crossed the gulf in the *Teal*, dinghy and plywood boat in tow. On board the *Teal* were heavy weights, ropes, and chains. These were the moorings for the *Teal* and dinghy. The plywood boat was to be the tender and would be left on the beach. Pop drove the Austin from Adelaide and they met at the Port Vincent cemetery, where they pitched a tent loaned by Norrie Rix. This was their base camp for the next few weekends.

In the weekends that followed, they explored the waters around Port Vincent. The results were disappointing, for they found nothing to improve on the catches they were already making off Outer Harbor. They looked for the Orontes Bank, but there were no boats to show them the way. They decided to explore along the coast, but do they go north, or do they go south? To the south was the coastal town of Stansbury, some 10 miles away. To the north, the nearest big town was Ardrossan, 27 miles away. Their experience at Port Vincent had convinced them that fishing close to a big town was no better than fishing off Outer Harbor. They decided to explore north.

12 INTO EMPTY SEA

The search to the north was slow and methodical. Each weekend, Pop and Frank would depart Port Vincent and pick up their journey from where they left it the weekend before. They stayed close to shore where they could see the bottom, for they had no sonar. Sonar for the weekend fisherman was something Pop never saw in his lifetime.

Pop knew that they had a problem, but did not know how serious. They were not sure what it was they were looking for. Their meagre experience had been gained on the metropolitan coast, and this place was different. They were beginners, learning on the job, with no one to teach them. They had so much to learn. It would have been easy, had they come across other boats, but there was just empty sea. They wondered if people ever fished this coast, or was it simply bad luck that there were no boats on the days they were out looking.

They looked for Whiting holes, like the ones they were familiar with on the Semaphore blue-line and around Outer Harbor. These were clear, sandy patches, easily distinguishable in the tape weed meadows. They found miles of tape weed, a few sandy patches, but very few Whiting. What they did find was large areas of hard, reef-type bottom, unlike anything they had seen before. They tried many times on the hard reef, and concluded it was not the type of bottom where they would find Whiting.

Finally, they came to a small town they assumed to be Port Julia. They hoped there might be at least one boat fishing off the town, but there were none. They pushed further north, finding more hard reef. It was while checking this reef that they noticed what appeared to be a mast in the distance. A boat at last. They set course for it, but as they drew closer, they could see it was too solid to be a mast. Disappointment set in, for there was no boat, only a pole standing in the water, about a mile offshore. None the less, it was interesting. Why was the pole there? They pushed on.

As they drew closer, they began to see sandy holes surrounded by tape weed. This was what they were looking for. Would there be Whiting in these holes? It was late afternoon. They chose a hole at random, for they did not know what might distinguish a good hole from a bad one. The hooks were baited and cast, and to their amazement, fish bit immediately. Every throw produced a Whiting, sometimes two. Whiting had never been so easy to catch. The bite continued to sunset, by which time they had all the fish they could handle. The place exceeded all expectation, but where were they?

The shoreline was by now a black silhouette, cast against the fading glare of sunset. The pole appeared to mark the end of a spit, similar to the one at Port Vincent. This spit also originated from a point of land at the southern end of a bay. They guessed the bay to be about three miles across.

They checked their map, a primitive road map picked up from a COR service station. The map showed a point of land and a bay, between the small towns of Port Julia and Pine Point. However, the map showed no roads accessing that section of coast. They needed more information if they were to set up a new base camp.

As it was too late to go ashore, they decided to stay the night. They made their way in, running along the bay's southern perimeter, which was by now, black and featureless. The profile of the land suggested an absence of cliffs, and they guessed from what they had noticed that afternoon, it was covered by dense scrub. There were no lights. The shore appeared uninhabited. Finally, about two miles from where they first pulled anchor, they came across a single light, possibly a farmhouse. Some distance north, they could see a few more lights, and guessed it might be the township of Pine Point. They anchored out from the single light.

Next morning, they rose early, and found that they were opposite a farmhouse. It was at a point where the scrub they had passed the night before, gave way to low cliffs. The cliffs ran north for as far as the eye could see. A short distance along was a small rocky headland, and further on, they could see a few scattered buildings. Probably Pine Point. Inland, was mostly farm paddocks.

Looking south, they saw only scrub. A narrow beach skirted scrub. It appeared similar to the Port Vincent beach, and was a little over a mile long. A good distance along the beach were two green sheds, strangely remote and isolated. An odd bit of civilization in the middle of a wilderness.

There were also several sheds on the beach adjacent the farmhouse, including two bathing sheds. A single shack sat at the top of the sand hill behind the sheds. However. it was the farmhouse that drew their attention. That was where they hoped to find their answers. They anchored the *Teal* closer to the beach and waded ashore.

The farmer was a lady, Amber Harvey. Amber had lost her husband, Norman, during the war, and had been left to run the farm on her own, as well as bring up son Brian and daughters Joan and Pauline. The Harvey's did not get many visitors and were not encouraging of strangers, for they had experienced problems in the past with spot-lighters on the property. When two scruffy, and claiming to be lost, fishermen, walked uninvited into their yard, they were not sure what to make of them. No vehicle, no spotlight, and no guns, helped the visitor's cause.

The lost fishermen were told that they were at Black Point. They thought it an appropriate name, given their first impression the night before. The rocky little headland nearby was called Rocky Point. They thought that was an appropriate name also. The small point to the south of Black Point was called Little Point. Also an appropriate name. When told the town to the north was Pine Point, Pop guessed it was a place where he would find a pine tree.

Their final question involved the directions to get to where they were. An odd question, seeing they were already there. It was a memorable first encounter for all parties.

Once the road directions were sorted, Pop looked for a suitable place to set up a base camp. To get there, they would have to follow the narrow dirt road that ran from the main road and ended at the farmhouse. The base would have to be close to where the road ended.

Pop chose a spot behind the shack nestled amongst the trees at the top of the sand hill, which was the only other dwelling in the area.

13 BLACK POINT

The following weekend marked the beginning of the Black Point campaign. Frank shifted the boats and moorings, while Pop set up a new camp. It did not take long for them to meet their only neighbour, Jack Fitzpatrick. Jack was a scrap metal dealer from Adelaide. He introduced his wife as Cookie and said they had three boys running about the place, somewhere. He warned that the boys had a reputation, and people were quick to blame them for any damage to property. I was destined to become the fourth member of this group, and I think their reputation was a bit overrated, but not entirely. No one has ever explained how Mrs Harvey's harvester happened to carve a figure eight in her crop one night. The identity of *The Phantom and His Mate* also remains a mystery. This duo was known to have left their calling card at one (possibly more) minor crime scenes. The Fitzpatrick kids denied all knowledge. All I know is that they never did anything that bad when I was with them.

Jack was owner of the only shack at Black Point. He was not a fisherman, but the guests who stayed with him were. Doc Savage was a regular. Doc was a tuberculosis specialist, a disease more common at that time than now. Doc had two boats. One was an 18-foot sail-cruiser called the Wayfarer. The other was the June, a 16-foot open boat built for fishing. The June had a small well, big enough for Whiting but too small for Snapper. Like the *Teal*, it also had a short mast that served no purpose. Doc moored his boats in the bay.

In the weekends that followed, Pop and Frank explored the waters around Black Point. At night, they slept in their borrowed tent. Only once did they have a problem. They returned one day to find the tent pole broken. The Fitzpatrick kids were rumoured to have used it as a fireman's pole, but nothing was ever proven.

Black Point lived up to its first impression. The fishing was good. They had no trouble filling their little icebox with Whiting each weekend. It was only when Frank mentioned to the Doc that their real interest was catching Snapper, that the little icebox came under serious scrutiny. Doc told him the marks to the Harvester, a fishing ground off Black Point that he considered to be better than the Orontes.

For those unfamiliar with fishermen's marks, they are trees and other features on land that can be lined up to triangulate a position on the water. Fisherman seldom rely on marks these days, for the GPS does the job for them.

The ground was called the Harvester because an old harvester had been dumped there some years earlier, taken out on the deck of the locally owned ketch, the *Annie Watt*. The harvester further enhanced what was already a very fertile reef.

At the time, Frank had no idea how valuable Doc's information was. Doc said the marks had to be kept secret, for they were known to only a few. Doc did not say who the few were.

It took just one trip to the Harvester to expose a problem. Pop needed a bigger icebox. The Harvester was all that Doc had promised, which meant they had to upsize everything as quickly as possible, for the Snapper season would not last forever.

Pop considered an icebox that could hold a quarter of a ton of ice would be sufficient. However, that meant other things had to change. A quarter of a ton of ice would have flattened the Austin in the driveway. But time was precious, and scrounging the second-hand car market would take time. Frank found a ute on display in a dealer's showroom and used his savings to buy it. It was a brand new, 1953, FJ Holden. The dealer said that it was one of the first utes to come off the Holden assembly line.

I still recall the night Frank brought the ute home. Lloyd was home at the time, and we could not wait to see it. We hung over the front fence, Lloyd saying. "Look for bright headlights coming down the road. That'll be Frank's new car."

Meanwhile, Pop went shopping for an icebox. In those days, most commercial fishermen had iceboxes that would fit on a trailer or small truck. They were large, homemade, wooden boxes, with a watertight lining made from sheet galvanised iron. Cork or seaweed served as insulation. Such iceboxes seldom came up for sale, but Pop was lucky and managed to find one. It soon had a new home in the scrub alongside Jack Fitzpatrick's shack.

The summer season of 1952-53 was the turning point. Pop found more than enough Snapper to pay the mortgage. So certain was he about what he had found, that when the *Teal* returned to Outer Harbor for its winter layup, Pop did not bother to fish the nearby Barker Inlet. Frank was free to play football on weekends, and Pop was free to watch him. The poultry farm in the backyard diminished to about 10 chooks, and the vegetable patch all but disappeared. The tenants in the flat were also told that their lease would not be renewed.

The spring that followed in that year, marked the beginning of Pop and Frank's first full season at Black Point, and they were gone most weekends. Mum became a fishing widow. I know little about what happened that season, but I know they caught lots of fish and they told me stories about big sharks.

My life was in Port Adelaide, where I had joined the Cubs in anticipation of one day becoming a Boy Scout. However, circumstances ended my grand aspirations. Pop (or perhaps it was Mum) decided that the whole family needed to be at Black Point. Happily, I gave up Cubs, as Pop was about to take us all on an adventure – and it was an adventure I would not have missed for the world!

14 WE ALL GO FISHING

Pop had discovered that fishing at Black Point appeared to end abruptly once autumn arrived. The Snapper disappeared from the Harvester, as did the Whiting from the spit. There was no reason to return to Black Point until the following spring. Frank had football to play, and Pop had football to watch. Pop was torn between Frank's team, Semaphore Centrals, and his beloved Port Adelaide Magpies.

It was in the winter of 1954 that Pop prepared for the whole family to be part of his fishing venture. He purchased a small, second-hand caravan that he would leave permanently in the scrub, about 30 yards from Jack Fitzpatrick's shack. The caravan would be accommodation for all of us, and the icebox would go behind. Mum and Pop would have bunks, Frank would sleep on the floor, and I would have a hammock slung from one side of the caravan to the other. No arrangement was needed for Lloyd, for he was seldom home. Lloyd mostly lived on ketches. At other times, he would travel the outback. His home visits were only to get well enough to be off again.

Pop also decided to address the problem of his two boats moored in the bay, and the tender pulled up on the beach. They could not be left to face the winter elements, unattended. The dinghy had been unsound since the day we first launched it. Frank's repairs could not fix all the leaks, and it had to be pumped out weekly. The *Teal* also leaked, and had other shortcomings. It was a good Snapper boat, but did not manoeuvre well when anchoring on small Whiting patches. The boats needed to be brought back to Port Adelaide each winter.

I recall well the night the boats made their final return crossing in 1954. That was the night Adelaide was struck by a 5.6 magnitude earthquake. Mum and I were asleep at home. Frank was with the boats, somewhere out on the gulf, while Pop was driving back in the ute. Suddenly, Mum and I were woken by the violent rattling of windows. Mum leapt out of bed to find her precious dream house shaking around her. The rattling continued for some time, our half-asleep brains trying to make sense of it all. Meanwhile, the fishermen were unaware that this historic event was happening. They arrived home next morning to hear our story, but we could show them no damage to prove our tale. Mum's dream house had stood up well.

The winter of 1954 gave time for Pop to solve all his problems. A well as buying a caravan, he decided that all three boats would be sold and replaced by a single trailer boat. The trailer boat with the highest reputation in Port Adelaide, was the Clausen. These boats were built in a modest workshop on Fletcher Road, not far from where we lived. Frank called on the boat builder and ordered a 14-foot hull, made from the thinnest clinker planking possible. There was to be no deck, as this would add weight. Keeping the weight down was a major consideration, for there was no boat ramp at Black Point. The only way to get a boat to the water was to manually push it over the sand.

Frank ordered just the basic hull, for he was relying on his handyman skills to complete the job. While waiting for the hull, he made a wooden trailer. Again, it had to be as light as possible. To maximise strength and lightness, the timber was laminated, and the winch, tow fitting, and fastening U-bolts, were fabricated in the aeronautical workshop of Vickers-Armstrong. Vickers-Armstrong was Frank's employer. They produced a number of the 20th Century's iconic aircraft, the most well-known being the Vickers Viscount. I believe, however, that they hold no official record of ever producing a set of boat trailer fittings.

Frank finished the trailer in good time to pick up the hull. Once the hull was home, he put in the floor and seats, then installed a 4-horsepower, 2-stroke, Penguin motor. After that, we all painted.

15 THE CLAUSEN

The Clausen made its debut in the 1954/55 summer season. During the week, it stayed under a tarpaulin in Harvey's farmyard, about 200 yards from a track cut diagonally down the cliff face. The track led to the beach. Today, a concrete boat ramp marks the spot.

Pop, Mum and I, welcome the arrival of the Clausen at Black Point. The caravan is in the back ground. Frank's Ute is there too, but Frank is hiding behind the camera. It was the day we all became part of Pop's Fishing World.

Each weekend, Frank would back the Ute and boat to the bottom of the track. That was the easy bit. Next came the hard bit, as the boat had to be manually pushed across the soft sand. Retrieving the boat Sunday afternoon was even harder. Once the trailer reached the water, wave action quickly caused the wheels to sink in the sand. Attaching a towrope to the ute would have been useful, but the track ran at right angles to the beach, which ruled out this option. Retrieval of the boat, bogged or otherwise, required a zigzag manoeuvre one wheel at a time. Even Mum was required to push. Some may have wished for a boat ramp, but we considered the lack of ramp to be a blessing. It was the reason why the Clausen was often the only boat out fishing.

The Clausen met all expectations, and handled the sea with flying colours. I recall an occasion when Frank and I were fishing together. Frank and I got on well in the boat provided our parents were not with us. With parents on board, sibling war always broke out. Siblings save their worst behaviour for their parents, but our parents had the answer. I was usually left onshore.

There were two boats on the water that day. One was the Clausen, the other, a two masted sailboat in the final stage of a gulf crossing from Port Adelaide. The sailboat had taken down its sails due to the strengthening wind and was relying on a small auxiliary for power. Unknown to us, it had gotten into trouble, and had sent out a distress call earlier that morning. It had run aground while attempting a short cut across the Black Point spit, and the receding tide had left it leaning on a dangerous angle. The crew was worried that as the tide came in, the growing waves might flood the boat before it could right itself.

All this had happened without us knowing. It was only when the rising seas caused us to head in from the Harvester, that we saw the sailboat's plight. We were headed for the spit just as the sailboat refloated, courtesy of the incoming tide. The flooding the crew had worried about did not happen.

The sailboat headed for shore, and we thought no more of it. We did not know that a large crowd had gathered on the beach. A crowd of any kind on Black Point beach was uncommon, but the bush telegraph had informed the district that a boat was in distress. Everyone came to the beach that day.

The crew of the sailboat came ashore, telling all that they were unharmed. Then they told of a small boat still out there, and it might be in trouble. It appeared to have been heading toward them just as they were leaving. They would have liked to have stayed to see if the boat required help, but were hampered because they only had a small auxiliary motor.

People scanned the sea with binoculars, and sure enough, from time to time they could see the Clausen bobbing in the waves. It was oddly lined up with the pole on the spit, and people assumed its occupants were somehow hanging onto the pole. How this would have been possible in rough seas is beyond me, but that is what some people were saying. It was assumed that we needed rescuing.

Fortunately, no one had any idea how to go about a rescue. The sea had already defeated the only big boat in the bay. Its auxiliary did not have the power needed to push out against the waves. Meanwhile, Frank and I were in the Clausen, catching Whiting. The spit sheltered us from the worst of the conditions, and we had no idea about the fuss onshore. Had Frank not decided to go in early, I am not sure what, if anything, would have happened.

We arrived back on land, to be welcomed by an unexpected crowd. We were asked lots of questions, most of which Frank deflected onto his nine-year-old brother, and I had no idea what all the fuss was about.

The Clausen well deserved the reputation it had earned around Port Adelaide and was now gaining at Black Point.

16 THE TRAPPER AND THE FARMHAND

At times we would arrive at Black Point and find the weather against us. For such situations, Pop had a backup plan. Black Point was overrun with rabbits, similar to how Pop had found Moulamein, 20 years earlier. Pop's backup plan involved the rabbits, but this time he had no need for a partner. I was drafted to be his assistant. I was not happy at first, but Pop soon desensitised me on the animal cruelty issue. He convinced me that trapping was a normal part of country life. Fortunately for the bunnies, this attitude does not prevail today.

Pop taught me everything he knew about trapping. I learnt how to run a string of traps so that the first few rabbits you caught did not frighten away the rest. I learnt to avoid trapping burrows with kittens, for the plan was to harvest rabbits, not reduce their population. Pop showed me how to use fresh earth to draw a rabbit to the trap. With me as apprentice, Pop made a concerted attack on those rabbits and would set about a 100 traps a night.

The rabbits, who were our victims, were gutted and left in their skins. Next, we joined their hind legs to make pairs. Then we slung the pairs over a horizontal pole suspended between two trees. Finally, we covered the pole and rabbits with a 10-foot long hessian bag, that Pop called a rabbit screen. Its purpose was to keep flies off the rabbits. Pop needed two rabbit screens for what he caught. Pop sold the rabbits. Fortunately, as Pop's fishing options grew, his preoccupation with rabbits waned. However, he always set a few traps, for we all liked a feed of rabbit.

Frank took no part in rabbit trapping, but he had a stint as a farmhand. It was late in 1954 when Frank did what everyone would like to do. He quit his job. He was sick of being an accountant, and was looking for something else to fill the next 43 years before retirement. It was no coincidence that his resignation occurred at the start of the Snapper season, but whatever he thought his plans might have been, they took an unexpected twist.

Frank took up full time residency in the caravan at Black Point. It was November, and the hard sands of winter had begun to dry out and soften. Frank bogged the ute alongside the caravan. With no one around to help, he went to the Harvey farmhouse for assistance. Help was soon back at the scene, but it was Frank's permanent residency that drew most attention. It was harvest time, and he was an able-bodied person living almost on the farmhouse doorstep. Workers were at a premium in the district. Frank was persuaded to help with the harvest.

The agriculturally rich district of Pine Point produced a bountiful harvest of wheat and barley, which made the town a very busy place. It would take several months to clear the harvest, during which time ketches were regularly lined up at the town wharf while trucks drove in and out of the busy grain stack yards.

Picture courtesy of Pam Harmer

Farm work was a new experience for Frank, who had only known study, office work, football, and fishing. Mrs Harvey soon had him driving the harvester, sewing the up the full bags, lumping them onto the truck, driving them to Pine Point, and then lumping them off the truck. At Pine Point, they were either loaded straight onto a ketch, or held in grain stacks for later shipment. Frank enjoyed his small taste of farm life, and had difficulty explaining to Pop why fishing was on hold until the harvest was over, even though it was peak Snapper season.

Frank drove a truck for Mrs Harvey during the busy harvests of 1954-56, when every available hand was needed to do the work.
Picture courtesy of Pam Harmer

Mrs Harvey, on the other hand, began to take a keen interest in Frank's welfare. She could not understand how this 22-year-old, a former student of the Adelaide's most prestigious private college, an accountant who had qualified while still in his teens, was living a hermit like existence in the scrub opposite her front door. Without his knowledge, she used her many contacts and found him a job with a local accounting firm. Frank recalls her excitement when she told him of this wonderful opportunity, and her disappointment when he told her he was not interested.

Frank had successfully upset Pop for not fishing, and Mrs Harvey for not putting his talents to better use. There are times in life when it is simply too hard to please everyone. Frank was on sabbatical, and for the time being, he was just going to please himself.

As a footnote to this part of the story, Franks' sabbatical did not last long. However, in the two years that followed, he arranged for his holidays to be at harvest time, so that he could again help with the harvest on the Harvey Farm, so much had he enjoyed the experience the first time.

17 A CUTTER IN THE BAY

By the end of our second season, we had become an accepted part of the small Black Point community. During the week, the Harveys looked after the Clausen, and on weekends when the beach was too rough for a boat to be launched, the Doc would sometimes lend us one of his. The Harvester provided all the Snapper Pop could handle, and often, the Clausen was the only boat out fishing.

However, nothing stays the same forever, and on a Saturday morning in January 1955, the harmony came to an end. We had driven in the night before and had not noticed a small truck with an icebox on the back. It was parked under the trees, not far from our caravan. As usual, Pop and Frank were up well before daylight, as they wanted to be on the Harvester by dawn. They noticed the truck on their way out, but took little heed, as they were in a hurry to launch the boat. It was not until they reached the cliff top overlooking the bay that their thoughts snapped back to the truck.

Anchored just out from the beach was a cutter. In the first glimmer of dawn, they could just make out the rigging, the forward cabin, the sheltered cockpit, and a large icebox on the deck. It was the Ena. The Mad Man of Outer Harbor had arrived at Black Point, and his truck was parked near our caravan.

All day the fishermen speculated on what this meant, and that evening, they rushed to speak to the others. They had to warn them that a mad man was about. Dismay followed when they discovered everybody knew Robbie. He had been away for a couple of years, but often made Black Point his summer base. He was a good friend, and everyone was pleased to see him back. Pop was asked how it was that he knew Robbie. It was an awkward question. It went unanswered. Pop was shocked that the mad man had friends, but even more shocked that we were camped in their midst. Pop had his own questions and they raced through his mind.

Was Robbie the reason so few fishermen were here?
Was this the unknown place Robbie disappeared to?

How difficult would life be at Black Point from now on?

In the weeks that followed, Robbie kept to himself. Each day, the Ena would disappear over the horizon and return well after dark. Robbie would take his truck down to the beach and unload his catch. We always knew when this was happening, for we would hear him crushing ice.

Curiosity eventually got the better of Frank. He had to know what Robbie was catching, and it would be easy to find out. Just wait until Robbie was gone, go to his truck, shift the tarpaulin, then lift the lid on the icebox - and that is what Frank did. He found the icebox to be three-quarter full of Snapper. Frank closed the lid, carefully putting everything back in place, so that Robbie would not suspect a thing.

However, Frank's plan had one failing. He had under estimated the craftiness of Robbie. When Robbie returned that night, he knew at once that someone had tampered with his icebox. Despite there being several possible suspects, not the least of which were the Fitzpatrick kids, Robbie immediately accused Frank. A classic Robbie verses Frank clash broke out. The normal quiet of the evening was shattered. Even the rabbits ran for cover. The exchange ended with Robbie considering himself the victor, for Frank could see no point in denying the charge. Instead, he expressed great admiration for Robbie's ability to catch so many fish, and hoped Robbie was pleased that he had left the icebox exactly as he found it. Robbie was not pleased. The incident just added fuel to an already existing war.

Robbie's run of Snapper continued for some time, and all the while we assumed he would return to Outer Harbor once it was over. This was not to be the case. In March 1955, we had our greatest shock. We arrived one Friday night to find Robbie's caravan parked close to ours. It appeared that Robbie had abandoned his Outer Harbor base and was setting up a new one at Black Point. The Mad Man of Outer Harbor, the fisherman who struck fear in the hearts of others, our enemy, was suddenly our nearest neighbour.

18 ROBBIE

It was with much relief that we discovered that none of our other neighbours would buy into the argument we had with Robbie. They all knew what he was like, and were not at all surprised that our relationship was on a war footing. Frank, to this day, describes the clashes with Robbie as *War on the Water*. Robbie was battling to hold territory he believed to be his, and we were the invaders. Fortunately, there was a battle line. Like sportsmen who are enemies on the field, Robbie was our enemy on the water. That was where the fight stayed. Frank's icebox clash was the only time the battle ever came onto the land.

The others told us that Robbie's main ground was a shipwreck in the middle of the gulf, but he had begun to loath the heavy seas he often had to pound through to get there. Recently, he had decided that it was time for him to fish the Harvester, for the shorter journey was less taxing on his aging body. When he discovered that his good friend Doc had told us the marks to the Harvester, he had been most upset.

I think there are few these days who know the history of the Harvester. I was told that the Rooney brothers discovered the ground in the 1930s. Sometime after that, I suspect they arranged for Reg Harvey, owner of the ketch *Annie Watt*, to have a derelict harvester dumped out there. Colin Rooney was a good friend of Robbie's and probably told him the marks. Robbie was a good friend of the Doc and told him the marks. Doc told us the marks.

The Harvester was the place where Robbie planned to fish in his old age. He never anticipated that the Doc would tell his enemies of its existence. Robbie had hoped to have the Harvester to himself, but Doc had changed all that. Robbie had come back to Black Point to start fishing the Harvester, and discovered Pop already there. The Outer Harbor situation would be happening all over again, only I was now old enough to at times be in the action.

Encounters with Robbie were regular occurrences when I first fished for Snapper with Pop. As a 10-year-old, I found Robbie's tirades a little disappointing. He was far less threatening than the character I imagined when I was five. There was no talk of guns, or ramming, or taking the food out of a professional's mouth.

If we got to the ground first, Robbie would usually bellow, "Yah got me marks taked pretty well agen, aint yah." Then he would anchor as close as possible, the massive hull of the Ena threatening to roll over our little boat if the sea was running high. The rant would continue. We would hear about his other ground, the one we guessed years later to be the Zanoni, though Robbie did not know what wreck it was. He only knew that it was an old ship with timber planks. Robbie called it his ancient shipwreck.

Robbie told us that he was only fishing the Harvester because of the discomfort he endured getting to his shipwreck. In his words, he no longer wished to *roll his guts out.* Then he would threaten how he might have to resume fishing his other ground, but first he would destroy the Harvester using Snapper Traps. Destroying the Harvester was the price he was prepared to pay just to get rid of us. I asked Pop what a Snapper trap was, but Pop had no idea. "You'll have to ask Robbie that one," he suggested.

Clashes with Robbie were many, but no harm was ever done. Talk about things such as Snapper Traps, simply left Pop and Frank with a large credibility gap where Robbie was concerned.

As time went on, Robbie's tirades diminished, until they were no more than odd outbursts of annoyance. Robbie appeared to mellow. We began to see the other Robbie, the one who was friends with all at Black Point but us. He had a sense of mystery about him. He knew the secrets of the gulf, for he had roamed its waters for many years. Some days we saw him fishing, other days the Ena would be gone, and we could only guess where it might be. I would love to have known all the things that Robbie knew.

19 THE MYSTERIOUS BLACK POINT SCRUB

In those early years, I was not required to be part of the fishing crew. I was left onshore, while the others went out fishing. To amuse myself, I would borrow Doc's 8-foot tender boat and do my own fishing. At other times, I would race my toy yachts, make sand castles, or snorkel close to shore. Often, I had the whole of Black Point beach to myself.

However, there were weekends when the Fitzpatrick kids would be over. Their ages ranged from eight to eleven. Brian was the oldest, then Normie, and Tyrone was the youngest. Normie was the ringleader, and had earned himself a bad boy reputation. I recall a fight we had not long after we met, though I cannot remember why we fought. Fortunately, Normie's mum was watching from the shack and noticed I was in trouble. She ran down to the beach and pulled Normie off me. By then, I had been pinned under the water for some time and was close to drowning.

To the best of my knowledge, no one told Pop about the fight. This was a good thing, for Pop encouraged his boys to fight. Fighting had been a necessary skill when he was growing up in a boarding school, and he would not be happy to hear that I had lost a fight with Normie. Ironically, after the fight, Normie and I became friends.

When the Fitzpatrick kids were there, we walked for miles. A favourite destination was the far end of Black Point. This remote spot was once considered the likely site for South Australia's first quarantine station, and nothing had changed in its isolation since then. To us, its lack of access made it a place of mysteries.

The first mystery to puzzle us was a tent we found hidden in the sand hills. Made from hessian, the tent was not waterproof. Strangely though, it had a sturdy timber frame more suited to a garden shade house, suggesting it was a permanent structure. The area was windswept, and there were no footprints in the sand. The tent was empty and appeared abandoned. We wondered who had put it there, and why. It had not been there on our previous visit, and when we returned a few weeks later, it was not there again. No footprints, no rubbish, nothing to show anything was ever there, only windswept sand. To us kids, it was a mystery, but we failed to enlist the interest of adults in solving it.

Kids love mysteries, even if adults are not interested. Our next mystery occurred close to the same spot. Occasionally, we would visit an aboriginal burial ground where bones sometimes appeared, exposed by the shifting sands. We would check to see if the wind had done its trick again.

On the day of this mystery, the air was still. Our voices and the occasional birdcall were the only sounds to be heard. Suddenly, as we approached the burial ground, a noise shattered the calm. A slow hammering came from somewhere ahead. We speculated that someone had hung a sheet of galvanised iron from a tree, but there was no wind to make it move. We wondered how a sheet of galvanised iron would come to be in the area anyway. The only building at the end of Black Point was a stone ruin, of which only the chimney was still recognisable. It was the original farm cottage, built by the Wheare family in 1889. The ruin, a freshwater soak, and the burial ground, were all in the same area.

The sound was eerie. There was no reason for anyone to come to the area that we knew of. We wondered who, or what, was making the noise, and the mystery remains. We headed in the opposite direction and I never went back to the burial ground again.

A third mystery happened about half way along the point. We came across a little girl about four years old. She was wandering through the scrub, neatly dressed, wearing a tartan skirt.

"Are you lost?" we asked.

"No," she said, and offered no further explanation.

We went to ask another question, but she walked away and disappeared through the bushes. We stood there puzzled, and then a young man appeared. I recall he was wearing well-pressed trousers. Both he and the girl appeared dressed for a day at the shops, not a day in the scrub, miles from anywhere.

"Have you seen a little girl?' he asked in a matter of fact tone.

"She went that way," we said.

"Thank you." And we never saw either of them again.

We looked around, but could not work out how they got there or where they were going. There was no boat on the beach, and we saw no car in the paddocks. There were cars back where everyone parked, but we knew the owners of those. Obviously, there had to be a simple explanation for this bizarre encounter, but we never worked it out. Possibly, they were a couple of beach walkers who had wandered into the scrub, though few people ever walked that far along the beach.

That was the only time I recall coming across people during one of our bush walks. We simply added the two strangers to our list of mysteries.

Not everything at the end of Black Point lacked explanation, however, but a lack of knowledge could have cost us dearly. At low tide, we would catch Blue-ring Octopus with our bare hands, and put them into glass jars. They were abundant on the reef, and no one knew that they were poisonous. Now, most people know that their bite produces a paralysis which causes death by suffocation. Fortunately, prolonged mouth to mouth resuscitation can save a victim, but there is no known antidote to the poison. Luckily, we were never bitten.

20 THE FITZPATRICK KIDS STRIKE AGAIN

There is one story I must tell about the Fitzpatrick kids that happened when I was not there. Thanks to them, Pop and Frank were not the only ones to be in Robbie's bad books. Doc owned a bow and arrow with which he planned to one day shoot a White Pointer shark. He suggested the idea to Robbie but was firmly told, "You won't be doing that off my boat". Robbie had his own method of dealing with sharks, far more effective than a little arrow that would only annoy them. It intrigued us that Robbie held Doc in great favour, and sometimes took him to his secret places. Doc had been to Robbie's shipwreck, and could vouch that it was alive with Snapper.

The deed that invoked Robbie's great displeasure began when the Fitzpatrick Kids discovered Doc's bow and arrow in the shack. The kids had all made bows and arrows from tree branches and straight bits of wood, but none had ever handled the real thing. They could not believe their luck. The bow was almost as tall as they were, and the arrows had sharp, steel heads for hunting. There were no adults around. It was a perfect opportunity to try their skills with the real thing.

They decided to start with a big target, and the biggest thing they could find was Robbie's caravan. They fired the first arrow, but the result was disappointing, for the arrow almost disappeared through the wall. Only the bit with feathers remained visible. The caravan was no good. They wanted a more solid target; one where they could see the whole arrow sticking out of whatever they hit.

Unfortunately, a problem occurred when retrieving the arrow. They knew it would leave a hole, but Robbie's caravan was far from new and they hoped a hole would go unnoticed. That was before the arrow broke off. Somehow, the steel head became stuck, and the arrow snapped as they tried to twist it out. Most of the arrow was retrieved, but not all. They decided it best they give up on bow and arrow practice for the day, and return Doc's possessions to their proper place. They also disposed of the damaged arrow, thinking Doc might notice it had a problem when next he came to use it. The only thing they could not fix was the damning piece of evidence left at the scene of the crime, but perhaps Robbie would not find it.

That night, as Robbie enjoyed his dinner, he looked toward the rear of his caravan, and there, just above his pillow, he noticed what appeared to be an arrowhead protruding out of the wall. On close inspection, he discovered it was an arrowhead, suspiciously like the ones on Doc's arrows. His caravan had been under fire. He finished his tea then called on Doc, for he needed to discuss the new feature decorating his bedroom.

Doc checked his stock of arrows, and yes, one was missing. Three suspects were quickly rounded up, and they pleaded their case. There were no witnesses, and no fingerprints. No court could convict them without evidence, but unfortunately, they had no lawyer. All three were found guilty and that night went to bed with sore butts.

21 HOW NOT TO KEEP A SECRET

It was a weekend in the spring of 1955 that Pop and Frank had their biggest catch on the Harvester. They thought it too early in the season, but it was such a calm night that they decided to try anyway. The Clausen was the only boat on the water that evening, and what happened came as a complete surprise. They found the water at the Harvester to be alive with Snapper. Their baited hooks barely broke the surface, before the line would rip through their fingers. It soon became obvious that they would have to stop fishing at some point, or they would sink the boat with fish. Fortunately, the calm sea enabled more fish to be taken on board than could otherwise be done safely.

They arrived back on shore to find everything in darkness. This was fortunate, for it meant they had a chance of keeping the early arrival of the Snapper a secret from Robbie. If Robbie found out, he would hammer the school and the fish would quickly become less cooperative. Waking the sleeping camp was not their only problem, however. Most of the fish had to be gutted, a job that would take some time. Then, there was the problem of storage, for they had too many fish for the icebox.

The only solution was to take the fish back to Adelaide and put them into the fish market, first thing in the morning. The ute was brought to the bottom of the track used to launch the boat, and the catch was loaded onto the back. A small space was left for Frank to sit. From there, he could work his way through the pile of fish, gutting as he went. The offal would go in a bucket and be thrown out at various points along the journey, giving the wildlife a change in diet from the usual road kill.

The plan started well, and the fisherman departed Black Point without waking a soul. Pop took the wheel, with Frank in the back. Unfortunately, Pop was unfamiliar with the task of driving and took a wrong turn. Instead of bypassing Ardrossan, he went through the centre of town.

When Pop Took Us Fishing

Darkened buildings alerted Pop to his mistake. He felt annoyed with himself, for this was no way to keep a secret. He looked anxiously around, but it was well after midnight and the townsfolk were all in bed. Pop was relieved. No one saw the strange sight of Frank sitting in the back with a pile of fish. The bush telegraph would not be telling Robbie that Snapper were about. But Frank was less observant. His head remained down, as he dealt with the job on hand.

It was almost sunrise when they arrived in the city, their long night's work almost done. Pop joked to Frank about his mistake, and how it could have exposed their secret, but fortunately, the Ardrossan folk were kept in the dark, so to speak. Frank was not so sure. Pop asked why. Frank then confessed that townsfolk would soon be waking up and wondering why they had Snapper guts strewn all over the footpath in the centre of town. He had chucked a bucket full out before realising where he was.

They returned to the Harvester the following night and repeated their effort. Over the two nights, they caught 106 big Snapper. This was the biggest catch Pop ever had at the Harvester, though he later had bigger catches elsewhere.

On the following weekend, they fished the Harvester again. Unfortunately, they discovered that Robbie had been fishing there all week. The secret was out. Pop never asked Robbie if he had heard about the Snapper guts. Neither did Frank.

22 ROBBIE THE WISE ONE

As time went by, the frosty relationship between Robbie and ourselves, thawed. Black Point was clearly the place where Robbie had planned to spend his remaining years. If his enemies could not be driven out, he would have to make peace.

Robbie was actually a good bloke to have around. The persona that had earned him his mad man reputation was mainly an act. It had served him well, turning away most of those who threatened to invade his private world. Unfortunately for Robbie, it had not turned us away, something he was slowly coming to terms with.

Robbie was the same age as Pop, slightly built, and very agile. His head was balding, and when he spoke, his eyebrows sometimes moved with an intensity that caught your attention. He was a good talker, and had an air of eccentric enthusiasm about him.

To me, Mad Man Robbie became Robbie the Wise One, for he knew things about fishing that no one else knew. When Robbie spoke, I listened. Robbie was secretive about everything he knew, but delighted at times in giving cryptic clues. To Pop and Frank, he had a credibility gap. They would listen to him on factual matters, but had little time for his obscure references.

However, Robbie knew he had a good listener in me, and enjoyed telling me things. He told me how fish moved with the seasons, and the links between fish behaviour, weather, and barometric pressure. He showed me the best way to bait a Snapper hook, and told me how he dealt with White Pointer sharks. I asked if his method killed the shark, and he said it did. It was surprisingly simple and best now forgotten, as White Pointers have become a protected species. He told me how he sounded the depths with a lead line, and worked out what was on the bottom by smothering the lead with sticky tallow. He told me how surface fish, sea birds, and dolphins, gave important clues on what was below. He told me how wave patterns sometimes indicate changes on the sea floor. He said that was how he found his ancient shipwreck.

Pop and Frank doubted the existence of Robbie's often talked about shipwreck, despite Doc's verification otherwise. Thirty years would pass before the Zanoni wreck became common knowledge, and I tell that story later.

Another thing Robbie talked about was the rare, Sundowner Whiting, caught only at sundown. On one occasion, Frank caught a four-pound Whiting at the Harvester, just on sundown. It matched Robbie's description of a Sundowner, being similar to a normal King George, only much bigger, and slimmer in proportion. Its markings were blue, but turned grey once the fish had died. Unfortunately, Robbie was not about at the time, and we could not confirm the fish to be what he called a Sundowner. The Sundowner Whiting remains a Robbie mystery. I believe a separate species has never been identified, but still I wonder.

Robbie seldom answered questions, but I always paid attention, for I found everything he said was interesting. A question that puzzled me the most was, *Why do fish never get lost?* The teacher at school had told us about Atlantic Salmon. They swim thousands of miles in the ocean and then return to the river where they were born. I wondered how they did this, and why it was that Snapper could always find the Harvester at sunset and sunrise.

My chance for an answer came when Robbie mentioned a fishing ground he was yet to find. He believed a ground existed between the Harvester and the Orontes. I asked why he thought that.

"Distance. Those two grounds are too far apart," was his reply. "There has to be a ground in the middle."

I was surprised that Robbie had answered a question and thought that I might have a chance to sneak in another. "Where would you look?"

Robbie smiled slightly, sensing that he was being probed for information. Then he answered.

"I would follow the line that joins them." His answer was matter of fact, as though he was telling me something everybody knew. The response puzzled me, but it was always difficult to gauge the things he had to say. He revelled in his vast fishing knowledge and liked to tease when rationing out scraps of information. I felt compelled to continue my dumb line of interrogation.

"How do you find the line that joins them?"

Robbie paused as he carefully considered if, or how, he might answer my question.

"I would follow the reef. All reefs in the gulf run in the same direction." Then Robbie told me the direction he would follow.

This was great information. I was learning something from the master. I asked another question, this time hoping I would appear a little knowledgeable.

"Are these lines between fishing grounds the pathways fish follow so that they don't become lost?"

Alas, Factual Robbie disappeared and Cryptic Robbie answered the question.

"There are many reasons why fish are never lost. Each reason you find, makes you a better fisherman. Once you know all the reasons, you will always find the fish."

Question time was over. Robbie had begun to talk in riddles, and it would be 10 years before I realised the significance of all that he had just told me.

23 ROBBIE'S DESPERATE PLAY

Making peace with Robbie was a good thing, but he still schemed ways to stop us fishing the Harvester. Some years earlier, there had been a tragic accident. Robbie's friend, Colin Rooney, had disappeared while fishing off Black Point. No trace of Colin or his boat was ever found. Colin often fished the Harvester, and Robbie made a point of telling Mum that he knew what happened to Colin. Robbie claimed that on a day when the water was unusually clear, he saw the actual harvester on the bottom, and there alongside was Colin's boat, obvious victim of Port Lincoln Tom. We all knew about Port Lincoln Tom, as he was well acquainted with Pop and Frank. Port Lincoln Tom was a massive, 22-foot, White Pointer shark that frequented the Harvester. Robbie went to great lengths to tell Mum the story a number of times. He hoped it would worry Mum to the point where she would stop Pop from going to the Harvester. All it did was widen Robbie's credibility gap.

Finally, it became obvious to Robbie that the Port Lincoln Tom story would not work. He had to try something else, but was almost out of ideas. He had just one card left to play. It was a card he was holding back, for playing it went against the very code of secrecy he lived by. It was a desperate play, but if it worked, it would turn us from Snapper fishermen, into Whiting fishermen. He had to tell Pop where to find lots of Whiting.

Robbie knew Pop had searched between Port Vincent and Black Point, but found very few Whiting until he got to Black Point. Robbie decided to tell Pop where he had gone wrong.

"Go south again," Robbie advised.

"There's nothing there, we've looked," was Pop's response.

Pop's lack of success would have amused Robbie. He continued with his advice. "Ignore the tape weed and sandy holes you think special. Look on the hard reef bottom. That is where you will find the Whiting."

Robbie went on to explain that the hard bottom was a summer home for Whiting; a place they took refuge in the gentle currents of the shallow water; a place where they could grow in the warm months of summer.

Pop queried Robbie again, for he had explored the hard bottom to the south and found nothing. Robbie agreed that the area gave the impression of being devoid of fish, but that was not the case. He then told Pop that there were places on the reef where he would find more Whiting than he could ever imagine. He just had to keep looking.

Robbie did not tell Pop exactly where these places were, only that they existed. Nor did he say how he knew about them, and the fact that Robbie was not known as a Whiting fisherman, put some doubt in Pop's mind.

Though sceptical, Pop acted on Robbie's advice, and after a number of excursions south, found two clear holes on the reef. Robbie had said that we should ignore sandy holes, but both these holes had Whiting. Pop named one the Big Hole, the other, the Neck. Between the two, they provided more Whiting than Pop could catch on the spit, but not enough to fill the icebox. He still had room for Snapper, and so he kept on fishing the Harvester.

Robbie's plan had failed, but then, on a Saturday afternoon, the unexpected happened. We were fishing the Neck. I was on board that day, as was Mum. Two was the preferred crew for Snapper, but four was good for Whiting. More lines in the water meant more fish in the boat. Mum was a permanent part of the Whiting crew, and I was sometimes drafted to boost the catch. It was a tight squeeze with four in the boat. Most fights between Frank and myself were over the limited space.

On this particular afternoon, we received a guest. We had never seen a boat in the area before, but suddenly we had company. A boat came from the south and anchored 150 yards from where we were. This was a surprise, for we had already looked where the boat was and found the reef to be no different to anywhere else. The Neck was the only feature in the area that gave some contrast.

To our surprise, the sole occupant in the other boat began to pull in Whiting after Whiting. Finally, we could stand it no longer. We anchored alongside. The fisherman introduced himself as Rex Tyrrell. He was a commercial fisherman from Port Vincent. His excursion that day was to see who we were, rather than make a catch.

"Looks like there are a few here at the moment," Rex said. "Might have to come back some time."

Rex came back a number of times that season. He would catch a few fish, shift inshore a little, then catch some more. His final stop would be about 100 yards from where he started. By then, he would have about 10 dozen Whiting. He never went over the same ground twice. Instead, once he finished his run, he would head back toward Port Vincent.

Rex never appeared bothered by us fishing alongside him. To the contrary, he seemed to enjoy the company. He told us many things we did not know. He told us that Whiting favoured different sections of the reef at certain times in the year. He told us the fish were on a four-year journey from their nursery at the top of the gulf, to the open sea at the bottom. In later years, I heard that scientists had confirmed this fact, but I do not think many knew it then.

Between Rex's Run, the Big Hole, and the Neck, we had plenty of Whiting to keep us busy. We had no idea why Rex's Run produced fish, or why the fish behaved the way they did. It looked no different to the square-mile of reef that surrounded it. The important thing was that Robbie's plan had worked, for Whiting often took up our entire icebox and trips to the Harvester became the exception, not the rule.

Rex never returned to his run after that first season. Some years later, we discovered that Rex and Robbie were well acquainted. Robbie was far from the reclusive character we first thought him to be. He had a wide network of friends, and they helped one another. Did Robbie ask Rex to go out of his way to ensure we found enough Whiting to keep us busy? I will never know. Such was the mysterious ways of Robbie.

24 SIBLING RIVALRY

It was on a family outing to the southern grounds that Mum declared us, and not Robbie, to be the fishing mad men. It all began a few weeks earlier during the school holidays. I was spending much of my time on the Semaphore Jetty with a friend, Peter Newmarch. Peter had invested in a shark line, made from heavy cord, with large corks spaced along it. The corks held the line near the surface, allowing the bait to be floated well out from the jetty.

Shark fishing off the jetty was a speculative pastime, but to our joy, a four-foot School Shark blundered onto Peter's line. We were two very proud kids, landing a shark in front of the many who strolled the jetty that warm summer evening. Following my friend's success, I invested in my own shark line, but had no luck - and worse was to come. That shark line was soon to get us all into trouble with Mum.

I was part of the fishing crew on the day Mum made her damning declaration. I refused to go at first, for I was sick of being runner-up in the sibling rivalry competition.

Pop, Frank, and me in the middle, with the Clausen. There was not a lot of room in the Clausen when we were all on board.

Mum had her special spot in the Clausen and none of us ever budged her out of it.

Frank and I fought continuously over space in the boat, and my big brother always won. Bribery was offered to get me on board.

"We will let you take your shark line. You will have a much better chance of catching a shark off the boat, than off the Semaphore Jetty."

I knew the offer had doubtful value, for Whiting fishing was always too intense for me to put out a shark line, but I agreed to join the crew anyway.

"Can I put the shark line out now?" was the question I asked all day. The answer was always, *No*, followed by a variety of explanations.

The fish are biting, or, *the fish have stopped biting, and we need to move on*, or mostly, *you can't do it now, your shark line will get in the way.*

My chance finally came when all fishing stopped, but by then, everyone, including myself, was tired and just wanted to go in.

It was on the homeward journey that a miracle happened. The tide was part way up, allowing us to cross the Black Point spit rather than go around it. As we crossed, I looked ahead, and there, about 80 yards in front was something I had not expected to see. I could not believe my luck. The fins of a shark, just like I had seen them in a picture show, and the shark was headed straight for us. Frank took over the shark line. He grabbed a squid head and baited the hook, ordering me to unwind line from the winder so that he could throw the bait into the shark's path. Pop cut the motor.

It was my shark line, but he had taken it over. No wonder there was so much sibling rivalry in the boat. However, the window of opportunity was short. There was no time to argue. My big brother had control.

It was then that things started to go wrong. A combination of wind and tide prevented the boat from coming to a stop. Meanwhile, I had trouble with the winder. I managed to get some line off, but then it tangled. Shark and boat were about to pass each other, too far apart for the line to reach.

Frank turned to me in frustration, demanding more line. He saw the tangle, thought for half a second and then yelled, "Follow me."

Frank jumped over the side and I followed, juggling the tangled line. The water was up to Frank's thigh, making it up to my waist. We waded quickly to where we would intercept the shark.

It was at this point that Mum began to yell. Mum was never known to swear, but she could put normal words together to make very effective sentences. I cannot recall exactly what it was she said, but it implied that we were stupid and were required back in the boat immediately.

But wind and tide steadily took the boat away, leaving only the shark for company, and it turned out to be much bigger than first thought. It was a Hammer Head, about 10 feet long. Mum's voice faded in the distance, her vocal tones now directed at Pop. She was telling him how important it was that he restart the motor he had foolishly shut down. Pop was thinking about how to do that, for Frank was the one who usually started the motor. Frank was thinking about how he was going to hold on to such a big shark, and I was thinking about how closely we resembled the shark's next meal. Only Mum had no need to think. She had already made up her mind that we were all a bunch of idiots.

This scene, which could have had a great climax, turned out to be a fizzer. Frank managed to land the squid head almost on the shark's nose, but the offering was ignored. The shark came within six feet of us as it swam by. It seemed oblivious to the fact that we were there. Pop got the motor started, and the boat returned to pick us up.

The balance of the trip home seemed to take much longer than usual, for we were lectured all the way. Frank was scolded for being so stupid, leading his little brother into such peril. I was in trouble for being silly enough to follow him, and Pop for allowing it all to happen. In defence of us all, Pop expressed his opinion that Hammer Heads were probably harmless, but Mum quickly threw scorn on Pop's credentials as a shark expert.

As usual, Frank was the winner, for I alone endured a consequence. My shark line was confined to the Semaphore Jetty, never again to be seen on the boat.

25 MUM SAVES THE DAY

From time to time, there were weekends when we should have stayed home. We would be fooled by a favourable weather forecast, only to find that the weathermen had got it wrong. Weather forecasters in the fifties had none of today's technology. Reports from ships passing through the Great Australian Bight would have been their best forecasting tool, but sometimes they lacked a ship when one was needed.

On weekends when conditions were too rough to launch the Clausen, we would hope the Doc was about and could lend us one of his boats moored in the bay. This was how it happened that Mum, Pop, and Frank were fishing on the southern grounds in Doc's boat the Wayfarer, when they were struck by *The Curse of the Westerly Wind*.

The Wayfarer was an 18-foot cruising sail boat with a cabin, a centreboard, and a full set of sails. It had a small auxiliary motor that was only useful on calm days. On this day, the motor managed the trip south, courtesy of a modest northerly blowing from behind. The plan was to come home later in the day, when the sea breeze came from the opposite direction.

Unfortunately, Pop was always the optimist where weather was concerned. A more experienced mariner might have known that the sea breeze was never going to happen. The wind swung, and *The Curse of the Westerly Wind* came back to haunt Pop again. Pop's previous battles with his nemesis had been on the other side of the gulf. On those occasions, big waves had driven the boat onto the land. On this side of the gulf, the westerly came off the land, and the Wayfarer was slowly being pushed out to sea. The anchor would not hold.

Frank went forward and hauled in the useless anchor. It was a hazardous exercise, as waves were breaking over the bow. They started the motor, but the boat went backwards, further and further out, into bigger and bigger waves. The sail was the only option, but no one had ever sailed before, and this was not a day for beginners. The conditions would have challenged the most experienced of sailors.

It is at times like this that personal safety comes to mind. The Wayfarer met all the safety requirements of the day. No life jackets, no flares, no radio. There were no safety requirements in those days. There was no safety network to rescue a boat, should one be in trouble. There was no way a small boat could let people know if they were in trouble. You were on your own. A boat in trouble either made it home, or sank to the bottom.

The first job for the novice sailors was to drop the centreboard. They noticed an immediate steadying in the boat's sideways roll. That was a good thing. Next, they studied the various ropes running down the mast. They found the one that raised the mainsail, and they hauled on it. Part way, they came across a line of short ropes attached to the face of the sail. These were reefing lines that could be tied to the boom, to minimise the area of sail in a storm.

What a good idea, they thought, as they tied the lines, setting the smallest sail area possible. However, even this little sail had the potential to capsize the boat, so strong was the wind.

They set course to the north west, the boat side on to wind and waves. Pop took the helm, Frank managed the sail, and Mum lay on the cabin floor. Her weight was needed on the windward side to help prevent capsize.

After much difficulty, they made it to the end of Black Point, but continuing around the point was well beyond their capabilities. They would have to leave the Wayfarer there for the night and return for it next day. However, they had one more problem to overcome. The centreboard prevented them from getting to shallow water. They raised the centreboard, but found they could no longer sail against the wind. They took down the sail. All they had to get them to shore was the little motor that had been running all the time.

The last 100 yards were an epic struggle. Each time the wind peaked, they would drop the anchor to prevent being blown out to sea again. It took some time to get to shallow water. Finally, they did, and the men jumped overboard and pushed the rest of the way. Once close to the beach, they dropped the anchor for the last time. A second rope was run up the beach and tied to a bush. This done, a relieved Pop carried Mum ashore, where he considered the crisis to be officially over, but he could do nothing about the long walk she had back to the caravan.

Doc got a shock when they all staggered in, bedraggled, and minus his boat. He listened as Pop explained the shortcomings of the vessel he had left tied to a bush at the end of the point. Doc was relieved that all had ended well, but concerned about his boat. Our little adventure left him wondering that perhaps Wayfarer was not a good name for a boat that went backwards in a storm.

That evening, Mum recounted the story to me. She described how difficult it had been for her to hang on in the pounding waves. She described how important it was that she retained her position to prevent capsize. She described how she had to stretch one leg out to the centreboard casing, to stop herself from rolling across the cabin floor.

Mum was relieved. They had survived a crisis, and Doc was not upset. Her mood tempted me to say, "It kind of sounds like Pop and Frank were the heroes Mum, you were just dead weight." My tongue was in my cheek.

Mum paused for a moment, as if to work out if they were my words, or if my brother had put me up to it. Then came her considered reply. "Possibly true, but sometimes the dead weight does a very important job."

26 PINE POINT

By 1955, Pop had become convinced that Black Point was a Fisherman's Paradise - without the fishermen. It was time for him to make a permanent base, as he did not intend to go anywhere else. Robbie's arrival had confirmed his opinion of the place, and the presence of his old foe did nothing to shake his resolve.

A boat shed on the beach was Pop's next project. It would house the Clausen, two double bunks, a table and chairs, and a bench on which to put a kerosene stove and hand basin. The table and chairs could be stacked to one side when making room for the boat.

Pop chose a spot at the base of the sand hill, close to our caravan. It was next to an existing shed that no one appeared to use. On the first weekend, we dug into the sand hill, making a flat area on which to build the shed. On the second weekend, we erected a timber frame that Frank had prefabricated at home. Completion was planned for the third weekend, but that never happened. A phone call received during the week from a councillor, indicated that Council was not happy with what had been done on weekends one and two. Someone had complained, and said they had fallen into our diggings. Weekend three was spent removing the frame and shovelling back the sand.

Pop was amazed that our activity in this remote location had come to the attention of the Council, let alone, that they would actually object to it. Whatever the reason for the setback, it proved a blessing, for it forced Pop to find another way to push his project forward.

What happened next could best be described as a rare meeting of Pop's two worlds. In the tradition of a true fisherman, Pop had become very secretive about his fishing. People in the city were only to know about the things he did in the city. Part-time professional fisherman was not an occupation that fitted well with a job that required him to associate with people who held important positions. Black Point also needed to be kept secret, for Pop feared a rush of fishermen would kill his Golden Goose, should they hear about all the fish he was catching. When any of us spoke about our weekends, we were forbidden to mention fish catches, fishing grounds, or the fish market.

Pop's secret fishing world was on Yorke Peninsula. Unfortunately, he knew no one who had influence with the Council there, but there were people in Adelaide who could help. He asked a favour. He wanted an allotment of Government land near Black Point. It could be land for lease or land for sale, but it had to be on a beach and accessible by motor vehicle.

A search through Government records identified suitable land on the shore of a little bay, north side of the Pine Point township. It was three miles from Black Point. Arrangements were made for four blocks to be surveyed. Pop and Frank were given the choice of a block each. They chose adjoining blocks, and the boat shed planned for Black Point was erected on the block chosen by Pop. A small room was added at the back. In this room, Pop put two iceboxes, the original from Black Point, and a new one, slightly larger. One box was for Whiting, the other for Snapper. Fish boxes used for taking fish to market were stacked in a corner, and Pop's collection of rusting rabbit traps was piled against the wall.

Pop's Black Point campaign was over in three years. September 1956, marked the beginning of his Pine Point campaign. It was a special beginning. At age 51, the country boy who was forced to work in the city was finally putting down roots in a country town.

Pine Point was a quiet little town. It sat atop a cliff overlooking the sea, and at first glance, was little more than open land with a few scattered buildings. All were dispersed along a half-mile of highway. There was a church, a hall, a schoolhouse, and a general store. A small factory where Bourne Engineering manufactured agricultural equipment appeared un-factory-like, housed behind a clean, white, masonry frontage.

Apart from the buildings, there were the stacks of bagged wheat and barley that flanked both sides of the main road. They were the town's main feature, standing like hastily assembled fortifications, as if to defend the town from an unknown enemy. There was no pub, and the town's few houses were either spaced along the main road, or scattered on Billy Goat Flat.

The wheat and barley stacks were an impressive sight.

Photo courtesy of Pam Harmer.

Billy Goat Flat was a sheltered stretch of land at the base of the cliff. At its southern end was the town wharf, where ketches docked to load grain. On the wharf was a red shed, the Flat's southern-most building. Half a mile to the north was our boat shed, the Flat's newest and northern-most building.

In 1956, Pop got his boat shed at Pine Point. He was finally putting down roots in a country town. Frank is seen here putting the final touches to the front doors. The place had no water or electricity, and I often got the job of emptying the chemical toilet.

The boat shed was located in a wonderful spot. We would wake each morning, the sun streaming through the screen wire door. Waves would be lapping the beach, the water only yards from where we slept. On one occasion, a storm surge almost drove the sea under the door, but there was nothing in the boat shed that the water could harm.

Mum would not have imagined that one day she would own her dream house and then spend the equivalent of a year of her life living in a primitive shed on a remote beach.

In this picture, our caravan from Black Point can be seen in the background. Mum had already spent the equivalent of six months of her life living in that.

The shore to the north of our bay was unspoiled and only accessible on foot. It was a great place to explore, with its narrow beach rimmed by multi-coloured cliffs. At low tide, there were tidal flats, and at high tide, the shoreline transformed to a series of little bays. It was a peaceful place, a pleasant walk, yet I seldom saw people there. I made new friends, Laurence and David Hale (possibly Hayles). Together, we explored the shoreline and cliffs, collected rocks, and hunted snakes.

The shoreline north side of Pine Point provided a pleasant walk, where I discovered multi-coloured cliffs and peaceful little bays. Walking the beach on this sunny morning (60 years later), is my daughter Karyn and my granddaughters, Sophie and Abbey. Abbey is the one wearing a dress.

Regrettably, the serenity of this unique place will be lost once the highway diverts around the 30-square kilometre Hillside Mine.

27 RON AND GLAD

When swimming in front of the boat shed, I was always on alert for crabs. Crabs, with their sharp claws, were an ever-present danger when swimming. From time to time, a group would come from Adelaide and raid the bay for crabs. They would cook their catch in several copper pots set up over campfires in the scrub. These crabs were destined to be sold in pubs back in Adelaide. After cooking, the crabs would be piled onto a tarpaulin and then distributed among the party. Sometimes, the pile would be two feet high and completely cover the tarp.

Apart from the occasional crabber, our area had two regular visitors, Ron and Glad. They were a pair of battlers in their forties, and we enjoyed their company. Ron was a barber by trade, but come noon on Saturday, he would rush home from the barbershop and hitch his 12-foot bondwood boat to his old car. In the boat was a small drag net, about 50 yards long. This done, Glad and he would be off to Pine Point. Sally, their overweight Jack Russell, would be on the back seat, along with a folded up and well used army tent. They had a permanent campsite in the scrub behind our boat shed.

On arrival, the tent would be quickly erected, and the boat dragged to the beach. Next, the net would be loaded onto a board placed across the back of the boat. They did this in a manner that would allow the net to peel off as the boat was being rowed. Everything was now in readiness. Ron would row to a likely spot on the beach. There, Glad would take one end of the net. Ron would row out, hoping to encircle an unlucky school of fish. The encirclement was complete once Ron brought his end of the net back to shore.

Once Ron was back on the beach, the net would be hauled in. Ron took one end and Glad the other. Anyone watching was welcome to help. I was Cork Boy. I helped Glad by hauling on the cork line at her end of the net. The cork line held the top of the net to the surface. Ron and Glad managed the lead line, which held the bottom of the net to the seafloor. The lead line took special care, for fish sometimes tried to escape under it. I was never allowed to be Lead Boy.

Compared to the catches we made from our boat, their catches were small. Ron considered a fish basket of Garfish or Mullet to be a good day's netting. Only once did he almost have an exceptional catch.

Ron had just run the net out, when suddenly, a boiling school of Salmon swept into the bay, slamming into the back of the net. They swarmed and splashed, as they fed on tiddlers that mistakenly thought they had escaped danger by swimming out through the mesh. Frantically, we hauled the net onto the beach and in our hurry to reload it onto the boat, ignored its meagre catch left flapping on the sand. Quickly, the net was on board and a breathless Ron jumped back into the boat. He was ready to entrap a couple of ton of salmon. He pushed out from the beach, and so did the Salmon. All Ron could do was watch them as they swam back out to sea.

Ron and Glad were a happy-go-lucky couple, partly explained by the empty beer bottles stacked at their campsite. Unfortunately, fishing requires a clear head. When rowing out with the net, Ron's judgement had to be precise. Go out too far and he would be stranded, with insufficient net to complete the loop back to shore. He would have to jump overboard and wade the rest of the way, dragging the boat and net behind him. When this happened, he would burst into song. Tony Bennett's hit song of 1957, "In the Middle of an Island", became Ron's signature tune.

To avoid wading, Ron had a rope that he could attach to his end of the net, but often the rope was not long enough. I recall an evening with a particularly high tide. Ron was his usual cheerful self, as he rowed out into the darkness. All we could see was the red glow of his cigarette. Ron often had a cigarette drooping from the corner of his mouth. When he rowed at night, Frank called it Ron's portside light.

None of us thought it unusual, when carefree Ron misjudged the distance and did not have enough rope to get back to shore. But Glad saw a problem. The water was deeper than usual, and Ron was a little bloke. Added to this, he was partially deaf.

"You can't jump out Ronnie, it's too deep," Glad yelled.

We watched the glow of Ron's cigarette. It moved to a higher elevation, indicating that Ron had stood up. It moved to the side, indicating Ron was about to jump overboard.

Glad realised that Ron had not heard. She yelled loader, "Ronnie, it's too deep."

But Ron did not hear Glad's warning. He made no reply. He just burst into song. "In the Middle of an Island."

We all knew what that meant. Ron was about to jump overboard and we could do nothing to stop him.

The song continued, "In the middle of –"

There was a splash, a brief silence, and the cigarette disappeared. Then there was more splashing, and swearing, and a short time later, Ron dragged himself onto the beach. The boat's anchor rope was in his hand. We hauled the boat to shore with the rope.

"You could have drowned you silly bugger," was Glad's only comment.

Ron said nothing. He had done it all before, and he would no doubt do it all again.

There were times when Glad would tell me about her brother, whose name, I think, was Arthur. Her brother had been in hospital since the war, but Glad hoped to one day have him home. The war had been over for 12 years, but Arthur believed it was still going on, and he could talk about nothing else.

I recall the time when Glad took him to Pine Point on special leave, but she only did it the once. I remember the day well. Arthur told me, in graphic terms, about the hardships he faced as a soldier in the Pacific conflict. He felt guilty that he was not with his mates who were fighting as we spoke. Later that day, he must have had an argument with Glad, for he came and spoke to me again. I remember him standing there, staring angrily toward the tent.

"If only I had me mates with me," he said. "We would run through that camp and kill them all."

Sadly, the war had robbed Arthur of any ability to enjoy life's simplest of pleasures. I never saw him after that day.

There was little we could do to help Ron and Glad with their hardships, but there was an occasion when Frank did help. We were returning from Pine Point one evening when to our horror, we came across Ron's bondwood boat, smashed to pieces on its trailer. The trailer had become unhitched in transit, and the boat had been wrecked. What was left was sitting at the Port Wakefield garage. Frank contacted Ron the following day. Ron was devastated. His Pine Point days were over. He could not afford to buy a new boat. Frank offered to help.

Ron brought the wrecked boat to our house, where Frank salvaged the keel and the transom. Around these, he built a new boat. All Ron had to pay for was the materials. Ron and Glad were back in business, thanks to Frank.

28 LEARNING THE HARD WAY

The one thing Pine Point lacked that Black Point had was a deep beach. Pine Point had a clean, sandy beach, about 20 yards wide, but water only reached it late in the tide. At low tide, our little bay was one large tidal flat, bounded by a reef, 400 yards out from the beach. Our boat had to be outside the reef well before low water.

Most days would see the fishing crew depart early, return about noon, ice down the catch, eat lunch, and then go out again. It would be low tide when they returned for lunch and there would be a lot of soft ground to walk through. A good morning would produce about 10 dozen Whiting, and carrying them in from the boat was always an effort. We knew the tidal flats well, as pathways had to be followed if you were to avoid the worst of the boggy parts.

The boat would be left anchored about 20 yards beyond the reef. My job was to watch the incoming tide, for it could be two or three hours before the fishing crew went out again. By that time, the boat would be in deep water and unreachable. I had to work the boat in with the tide to make sure this did not happen.

I cannot remember what distracted me one hot summer afternoon in 1957, only the outcome. A neglect of duty resulted in the tidal flat being covered by the time I checked the boat. I ran to the water's edge. It had just reached the beach. I calculated from this, that there would be three feet of water on the outer reef, and more than that under the boat.

I looked out and could see the Clausen bobbing on a sea of brilliant blue, yet to be troubled by the afternoon sea breeze. It made a pretty picture, but did nothing to lift my spirits. I had a long way to wade, but fortunately, the water was warm. I set off.

First, the water was ankle deep, then knee deep, then thigh deep, until I reached the reef, where it was waist deep. Perhaps not waist deep to an adult, but I was smallish, and it was waist deep.

I stood on the reef, watching the boat yaw back and forth on the anchor rope. Like a huge floating pendulum, it swung in repetitive cycles, out to sea, into shore, then out to sea again. I waited for the optimum moment when it would turn outward, for at that point it would be closest, and the stern in the best position for me to clamber on board. It was a good plan, but one I was soon to abandon.

I watched the boat complete an outward swing. Small waves lapped silently against its shiny white planks. I stood there, admiring how they glistened in the afternoon sun. In less than a minute, I would be on board. I just had to wait for the boat to swing back close. It was then that I noticed something out the corner of my eye. There, about six feet in front and just a little more to the right, was a 10-foot Bronze Whaler shark, swimming peacefully along the reef, and about to cross between me and the boat.

I had three choices. The first was to stand there and hope the shark would swim quietly by, as the Hammer Head had done at Black Point. The second was to turn back to the beach, but that was a long way to wade with a shark in pursuit. The last was to make a mad dash for the boat.

I chose option three, which meant crossing the intended path of the shark and possibly brushing its nose. It was probably the dumbest of the three options, but the boat looked so safe and so close, I just had to get on board. My focus was totally on the boat. I did not look at the shark.

I rushed forward but only managed a few steps before the sea floor dropped away; for once off the reef, the water was deeper. It seemed almost as deep as I was tall. I began to swim, though frantic threshing would better describe my effort. Finally, I touched the boat, not at the stern as planned, but mid-ships. I reached up and grabbed the gunwale. I knew hauling myself on board from there would be a struggle, for the stern was the only place that offered a footing. I was wrong. From somewhere, I found super human strength and cleared the side of the boat like an Olympic pole-vaulter. Next thing I knew, I was lying face down on the floor, not knowing exactly how it was I got there. The only thing I could recall for certain, was a brief feeling of relief, as my legs came out of the water without a shark attached.

I jumped onto the engine box. From there I could see 100 yards in all directions, for the water was crystal clear. There was no shark. It had gone. To be out of sight in such a short time meant our frights had been mutual. Like me, it had panicked, but it was dumber than I was. It had made a very poor error of judgement, and left untouched the best meal it was ever likely to chew on, and I was so glad about that.

Rightly or wrongly, swimming in our little bay became more enjoyable after that, as I worried less about sharks. I thought of them as big fish, easily frightened away, though still worthy of respect. They hunted at sunrise, sundown, in dirty water, and in moonlight. When conditions were dull, I was cautious. I knew differently about White Pointers, however. They were dangerous at any time, but fortunately, never came into the bay.

It had been an eventful day. Always keep an eye on the tide was a lesson well learned. The day had taught me more, however. I now had a new relationship with sharks, one that made swimming more enjoyable. My fear of them had waned. I just hoped that sharks would always respect our new relationship and never let me down.

29 LLOYD TAKES CHARGE

Among the first people we met at Pine Point was Captain Mick Buttfield. Mick was a recently retired ketch captain, and owner of a magnificent cutter. The cutter was new, built in Port Adelaide under Mick's watchful eye. It was the boat he planned for his retirement; similar to Robbie's cutter, only slightly smaller, but with a taller mast, for Mick loved to sail.

The sight of Mick sailing out from Pine Point had become a familiar one. Pop imagined how good it would be to own such a boat. He could stay out on the Snapper all night, the fish kept alive in the well. There would be no more rushing in to ice down the catch, getting three or four hours sleep, then rushing out again before dawn. There would be no more dragging large quantities of Snapper over the tidal flats. A cutter had long been one of Pop's fantasies, and when Mick announced that his cutter was for sale, the fantasy took hold.

The year was 1958, and four thousand miles away, the 490-ton Ian Crough was about to be launched from a Hong Kong shipyard. This brand new ketch would be the flagship for the Crouch fleet. Mick was giving up retirement to be its skipper.

Pop's dream to one day own a cutter, became a reality. Eleven years earlier, buying any boat had been a difficult decision. Pop's first boat, the pram, had been a luxury hard to justify. However, priorities had changed since then. Boats were now a major contributor to family income. Since the pram, Pop had trialled a bondwood boat, the 12-foot carvel planked dinghy, the *Teal*, and the Clausen. Mick's 22-foot cutter would be trial boat number six.

Pop thought that this time he had got it right. The cutter had everything that Robbie's Ena had, except a name. This was unusual for a boat its size, but Mick had not given it one. Pop wanted to give his boat a name. Several were debated, but a family consensus could not be reached. Pop liked the name Marlin, but no one agreed. The cutter remained nameless, and like Mick, Pop simply called it the cutter.

As a footnote to this part of the story, two tragedies followed shortly after Mick's decision to return to sea. The first involved Mick himself. We heard he was appointed acting captain of the *Claire Crouch* while waiting for the Ian Crough to be delivered. Unfortunately, the Clair Crouch struck a fierce storm somewhere off the Tasmanian coast, and Mick died from a heart attack while struggling at the helm. However, there was a second tragic event that overshadowed Mick's passing.

On the 26th September, 1958, the *Ian Crouch* sailed out of Hong Kong. She was on her maiden voyage, destination, Port Adelaide. The radio operator made a routine radio call the following day. That was the last contact ever made. The vessel vanished with a crew of 12, and the disappearance remains one of the great maritime mysteries. Many thought pirates were to blame. Nine of the crew were from South Australia.

The cutter was an exciting acquisition for Pop, and he was keen to take her to sea. However, circumstances saw the pleasure of the first cruise go to his three sons. Mick had taken the cutter back to Port Adelaide, as he had not expected to find a buyer in Pine Point. It was moored at Central Slip, upriver from the Birkenhead Bridge. Frank and I were tasked with taking it back to Pine Point. It would be a night crossing, and we would make landfall early the next day.

Frank had one worry. He had on many occasions passed under the Birkenhead Bridge, but the tall mast of the cutter required the bridge to be open. He had no idea how this was made to happen. Brother Lloyd, with his vast experience on ketches, said it was not a problem and was quickly drafted onto the crew.

That night, the three of us boarded the cutter and began the journey. Blackened wharves lined both sides of the river, the thumping of the cutter's motor the only sound to be heard. In front, we could see the streetlights on the Birkenhead Bridge, their reflections trailing across the water like ghostly fingers reaching to our bow.

As we drew closer to the bridge, we could hear the sound of traffic passing over it. With 50 yards to go, Lloyd directed Frank to idle the motor. The bridge looked daunting, towering high above us, the dull glow from its collection of lights falling faintly on our deck. The cutter showed no lights, for only very large vessels had navigation lights in those days. Frank and I wondered if those in charge of the bridge would look down, and if so, would they see us? That was when Lloyd took charge.

Lloyd jumped onto the deck. I could see in the dim light that he had a slight smile, but was trying not to show it. He went forward and stood on the roof of the cabin, one arm hanging onto the mast. Frank and I looked at each other, wondering what he was going to do.

With his free hand cupped to his mouth, Lloyd faced the operator's tower and bellowed out one long and very loud, "HOY." This he followed with three shorter, but equally loud, "HOYS".

It was the letter B in Morse Code, but would anyone take notice? Frank and I looked at each other, bemused. I could tell that Frank was hoping Lloyd's plan was better than this. Someone shouting at the bridge out of darkness was not going to work.

Suddenly, there was a booming reply from the bridge. It was as if a giant musician above us had decided to play one soulful but deafening note on his tuba. It fractured the silence of the river as it spread across the water, a faint echo bouncing back from the blackened wharves. Frank and I looked at each other again. We were speechless.

Next, we saw the glow of red lights flashing at each end of the bridge, accompanied by the sound of warning bells. Shortly thereafter, all traffic stopped. Finally, we heard a whirring sound and some loud mechanical clunks. The bridge began to open.

Lloyd came back to the tiller looking rather pleased with himself. "If I told you that was how it is done, would you have done it?" he asked.

Neither of us replied. We continued onward, down the Port River, Lloyd showing how each section was navigated by lining up red beacons he called lead lights. Frank had travelled the Port River many times, but not once had he ever taken notice of the lead lights. However, Lloyd was on a roll, and on that night we lined up every lead light as if the cutter had been a mighty cargo ship.

Unfortunately, our arrival at Pine Point next day was much later than expected, for we got lost. How this could happen with Lloyd on board would take some explaining, especially from the experienced mariner himself.

Throughout the night, Lloyd had picked a star on the horizon, checked it with the compass, and steered for it. He was confident he had held a good course. There was always a chance of a slight error at the end of the journey, as tidal movement in the gulf could cause a slight sideways displacement. But we were not slightly displaced, we were lost.

We discovered the problem at sunrise, when we first glimpsed the Yorke Peninsular coast. It appeared as a hazy grey cloud on the horizon, with one section lighter than the rest. The lighter section we guessed to be the cliffs of Port Julia. We were further south than we should be. We corrected course.

As the light grew better, we took a bearing off Mount Lofty, but it made no sense at all. We motored on until the town of Ardrossan came into view. We were too far north, not south. What we thought were cliffs at Port Julia, were in fact cliffs north of Pine Point. Our navigator had let us down, but he in turn was looking at the compass. He proclaimed it to be a dud.

Our position now known, we anchored much later than expected, about 800 yards out from the boat shed. That was where we planned to drop the mooring. It consisted of two train wheel rims that weighed almost a quarter of a ton. A crane had been used to put the mooring on the deck the day before. Our job was to push the mooring over the side without damaging the boat's exquisite timberwork. Mick would be upset if he were to hear that we had damaged his prize boat on its first outing. Happily, the exercise was completed with nothing bad to report to Mick.

With the mooring no longer on board, Lloyd noticed an immediate change to the compass. It began to behave as a compass should. The mass of iron on the deck had thrown it out. Lloyd breathed a sigh of relief. The compass was the guilty party. His reputation as a mariner was intact. He may have ranked last in the pecking order of family achievement, but navigation was one area where he felt he could shine.

30 THE SHARK SHOW

The purchase of the cutter marked a new era in our Snapper fishing. For the first time we had a boat bigger than the sharks. We had often looked toward Robbie's cutter, thinking how safe he was, as we kept a wary eye out for the sharks that regularly grabbed Snapper off our lines. Swimming to the safety of Robbie's boat was our only plan should one of these monsters ever misjudge things. We had no plan for the times we fished alone. A six-foot shark we could handle, but most were much bigger than that.

Bronze Whalers were the main worry. They would go manic, ignoring all rules of normal fish behaviour. Every fish learns from an early age that their world ends at the surface. Not so for the stupid Bronze Whalers. If they were chasing a fish headed for the surface, they kept on going. At times, they would rocket from their world, their short journey in space ending with an awkward splashdown on re-entry. It was something you had to be alert for when landing a Snapper.

White Pointers were different. They respected the rule that fish belonged in the sea. If they were chasing a Snapper and you managed to lift it out of the water, they were happy to let you have it. They went back and waited for the next. They presented a different problem. They were much bigger than Bronze Whalers, and could come from any direction. If a White Pointer were to accidentally ram the boat, the result could be catastrophic.

In all our years of Snapper fishing, we never had a White Pointer so much as brush the boat by accident, but Bronze Whalers were clumsy. We had a number of close shaves with Bronze Whalers, including one that did come on board. That story later.

A reference book I have always used is "The Marine and Freshwater Fishes of South Australia", put out by the South Australian Museum It describes all fish known to be in South Australian waters. Bronze Whalers are described as growing to about 10 feet long. I often wondered about that statistic. We regularly saw two Bronze Whalers at the Harvester that were 12 feet long, and would have been double the weight of a ten-foot shark.

It was while fishing from the safety of the cutter that one of these sharks gave me my second lesson in Bronze Whaler behaviour. My first had been while wading out to the Clausen. That encounter left me with the impression that Bronze Whalers were rather timid.

It was just on sundown, and Pop and I were standing at the back of the cutter, each holding a hand-line. A strong current was pulling the lines well out from the boat and large clumps of seaweed were going past in the current. Below the clumps, we could see little fish sheltering, and so could a school of hungry Snook. The Snook were ruthless as they attacked the small fish, their ferocity easily explaining why there were one-legged seagulls back on the beach.

We watched one clump go past with Snook muzzled into it as they tried to extract their sheltering prey. Suddenly, the water exploded and from nowhere, there was the monster Bronze Whaler, standing on his tail with the clump of seaweed and Snook in his mouth. Next came a huge belly-flop splash. The shark went on to attack several more clumps of seaweed.

Eventually, the sideshow ended, or so we thought. We continued holding our lines, waiting for the Snapper to make their evening appearance. Then the shark reappeared. It swam past the stern, Pop's line brushing gently along its back. The shark felt the line and with excellent peripheral vision, checked behind while still swimming forward. How it did that without a rear vision mirror, I am not sure.

At that precise moment, a single strand of seaweed being swept along by the current, struck Pop's line and came to rest. The seaweed's sudden stop was something unnatural, and the shark saw it. Instantaneously, it threw itself out of the water in a back-flip motion. It came down, the hapless piece of seaweed, no bigger than a shoelace, fell victim in its jaws. The shark's athleticism was incredible, its accuracy of attack amazing, but the stupidity of what it had just done was what impressed us the most. I quickly learned that when Bronze Whalers are feeding, they are irrational, unpredictable, and very dangerous.

This episode also annoyed Pop. A 200-pound, catgut hand-line, was our preferred Snapper gear. It was difficult to tangle, easy to grip, and could handle big snapper, two at a time. Pop had his favourite, and that was the line that had just brushed along the shark's back. When the shark grabbed the seaweed, it bit Pop's line in half, though half is perhaps the wrong word. Pop was left holding a useless 10 feet, the rest lost to the sea. Just one more reason for Pop's dislike of Bronze Whaler sharks.

31 THE WEST WIND STRIKES AGAIN

Fishing from the cutter was fishing in luxury. No more wet clothes, for there was none of the spray that drenched us in our smaller boats.

After four years of all being crammed into the Clausen, the cutter was a luxury. There was plenty of room to walk around on the deck. That's me hanging onto the boom.

Nor did we worry about being caught in a storm, for the cutter could handle the worst a storm could muster. The deck was another bonus. There was plenty of room to walk around, and if the fish were not biting, there were places where we could stretch out and relax. On a hot day, I would sometimes cool off in the well. The well was partitioned into two halves, and if one side were vacant, I would jump in. From there, I would sit with water up to my neck and watch the fish on the other side of the partition. The well was also home to three baby sharks I kept as pets. They had been born there, and I did not have the heart to tell them what it was we did with their mother.

However, nights were the most memorable. Being rocked to sleep in the forward cabin, waves lapping against the timber planks, the sea only inches from my head. There was the slight musty smell, and the all-night creaking of the anchor rope against the fairlead. To me it was heaven. Unfortunately, there were fewer of those nights than planned, for it meant leaving Mum alone in the isolation of the boat shed.

I recall rising one morning with Pop calling out, "Have a look at this bloke." I expected to see another boat, but he was pointing at the water. Lying alongside was a White Pointer, about 16 feet long. It had probably been there all night and showed no sign of going away. It could smell Snapper, and they were in our well. The smell was escaping through the circulation holes in the hull.

That was the day Pop discovered the problem with having a well. Robbie had told me he sometimes had this problem, and the simple method he used to deal with it, but his method is best not talked about. As much as we resented White Pointers for the odd times they interfered with our fishing, Pop would never risk upsetting them.

Unfortunately, the cutter's ability to attract sharks was not its only problem. An inevitable event soon exposed another. Mick had set the cutter up to be a sailboat, but sailing was something we had no time for. The motor provided ample power to get us to our grounds. However, *The Curse of the Westerly Wind* exposed a weakness. It happened on a day when we were all on board. It was as if Pop's nemesis had discovered the double bonus of striking when Mum was there, for Pop would wear Mum's displeasure for his poor judgement of weather.

We were at the Harvester when the same scenario occurred as had struck the Wayfarer three years earlier, but this time it was happening a lot further out, in much bigger seas.

Fortunately, the cutter was too big for the sea to be a danger, but like the Wayfarer, its motor struggled to make headway into the waves. Pop had solved the problem on the Wayfarer by using the sail, but the cutter's sail was stored in the forward locker. The motor was the only option. Luckily, we managed slight progress at full throttle, though a fit frog would have swum to shore quicker. It took several hours to get in, by which time it was late afternoon, and the wind had begun to subside anyway.

Normally, we would take the fish out of the well once the boat was back on the mooring. On this day, the slow trip in meant we had to do the job in transit, for the fish had to be gutted, packed, and taken to the fish market that night. Frank and I began the job midway into our journey.

In order to keep the boat wholesome, fish cleaning was always done on deck. This prevented messy liquids getting into the bilge, for such a mess would quickly result in a very smelly boat. Fish cleaning was not a difficult task, but this day proved the exception. It was impossible to stand on the deck. The boat pitched from side to side and stem to stern. Added to this, waves would come over the bow, run down the deck and then spill out over the sides. Staying on board was a job on its own. Losing fish over the side was a secondary consideration.

Frank's struggle with the Snapper on deck was brutal. Anglers know what it is like to handle an exhausted fish just landed, but a fully rested 20-pound Snapper plucked from a well, has all his fight still in him. Added to this, the cutter had no safety rail to stop Frank from sliding over the side, and the pitching deck was slippery with Snapper blood.

I was safe for most of the time, for I stood on the partition in the well. From there, I netted the Snapper and passed them up to Frank. Meanwhile, Frank braced himself, with one leg stretched out to any fixture within reach. In his right hand, he held a sharp knife; with the other, he wrestled the struggling fish. With both hands fully occupied, he had no way of hanging on. Staying on board was a priority, but cutting himself was also something to worry about. Fortunately, once the isthmus at the gills was severed, the violent part of the struggle was over. Frank gutted each fish and then slid it along the deck to Pop. Pop was standing in the stern cockpit, where he packed the fish into chaff bags and then laid the bags on the floor. Mum held the tiller and steered.

Finally, the Snapper were done, but one problem remained. There were three School Sharks in the well, each about five feet long. They were partitioned off from the Snapper, for Snapper tended to stress in the company of sharks. Sharks were a by-catch of Snapper fishing, and worth keeping, as they sold well in the market. My job was to get the sharks out of the well with a net that did little more than cover their heads. Like the Snapper, they were full of fight, but much stronger. Sharks also have the ability to twist their bodies, making them difficult to handle. Frank and I had worked out a method for handling sharks, but on this day, it required modification.

Normally, I would stand on the partition and put the net over the shark's head. Frank would then take the net handle while I reached down and grabbed the shark's tail. The two of us would then lift the shark to the deck where Frank dispatched it. Unfortunately, this was not a day for wrestling sharks on deck, the sharks had to be dispatched prior to then.

As always, I began by putting the net over the shark's head, but then came the modification. I jumped in with the sharks and put a full bear hug on the one wearing the net. My objective was to get its head within Frank's reach. Frank was waiting with a large mallet. Robbie had taught us about the sweet spot on the point of a shark's snout. Hit the sweet spot and the shark goes out like a light. Frank whacked at the writhing head until the sweet spot was found. Meanwhile, I kept my head away from the swinging mallet, and the rest of me away from the shark's teeth. The other sharks splashed in the well, but otherwise, were not a problem. They were not smart enough to realise they were next.

That night, as we drove back to the city, a family conference was held in the cabin of Frank's ute. I was not involved, for the cabin only held three people. I was in the back with the fish. On arrival, I heard the bad news. The cutter was to be sold. The experiment that was boat number six was over. It had lasted barely a year, and several factors were to blame for its failure. Maintenance cost, poor manoeuvrability, and the problems with handling a live catch, were all issues. But I saw another culprit. I believed the events of that day quashed Pop's fantasy for owning a cutter. Our luxury fishing was over, and I blamed *The Curse of the Westerly Wind*.

Frank and I had the job of taking the cutter back to Port Adelaide. I was dreading the Birkenhead Bridge. Lloyd had shown us what to do to make the bridge open, and I was hoping that Frank would not make me do it.

Prior to setting out, we took the main sail out of the forward locker and laced it back on the boom. We thought it might be a good selling point. It was on the second hour of our journey that Frank said to me, "Let's see what she sails like."

We hoisted the mainsail for the first time since we had become the owners. It was then that we realised how hard it must have been for Mick to part with his boat. She sailed beautifully, gently heeled over in the light morning breeze. We sailed on for several hours, until the breeze strengthened to a point where we lost confidence as sailors.

The other event I recall from that last voyage was coming across a large school of Tuna. We tried to catch them, but our Snook lines were no match. The Tuna smashed the lines as soon as they hit the water. Tuna schools often ventured into the gulf before the advent of our Tuna industry. Few people bothered with them. They were left to roam along the metropolitan coast, accompanied by flocks of seabirds that fed on the small fish the Tuna chased to the surface.

We arrived back at the Port, and the Birkenhead Bridge was not a problem. They raised it when they saw us coming; something we never told Lloyd.

The cutter was advertised and soon had a new owner; a crayfish fisherman operating in ocean waters off the State's southeast coast. We heard he replaced the motor with something stronger, which came as no surprise.

The cutter when it came back to Port Adelaide at the end of its first and only full season. The Birkenhead Bridge can be seen in the background.

32 LUCKY SEVEN

For several years, Pop and Frank would often fish all day without seeing another boat. By 1959, however, other boats were beginning to appear regularly. People were discovering Black Point, and the road that had stopped at Harvey's farmhouse was extended to the far end of the point. Over 100 shack sites were surveyed along the Black Point beach. Frank was among the first to secure a block, and he persuaded his friend, Don Fletcher, to be his neighbour. They both commenced building, and Frank's new shack had far more comforts than the Pine Point boat shed. Black Point had electricity, and there was a promise that mains water would soon be available. It was then that Frank announced he would be leaving the fishing crew.

Frank had a favour to ask when he broke his unwelcome news to Pop; he wanted to take the Clausen with him. Pop was happy to agree, for Pop had yet to find the perfect boat he wanted. The Clausen was a light boat, purpose built for launching from the Black Point beach. Also, it needed to be stored under shelter in order to preserve the integrity of its clinker planking. Pop wanted a more robust boat that he could leave on a mooring; one that offered more safety when big sharks were about.

Fortunately, Frank's shack took several months to build, giving Pop time to find the exact boat he wanted. What Pop found was the much-loved project of an amateur boat builder. Unforeseen circumstances had seen the project unfinished and abandoned. Pop was impressed by its workmanship and the quality of materials that went into it. Important components of the frame had been hewn from mangrove trees, considered the ultimate timber for such use.

A retired boat builder who lived not far from home was commissioned to finish the amateur's work. It was Pop's seventh boat, and this time he got it right. Had Pop given this boat a name, Lucky Seven would have been the appropriate choice.

Lucky Seven replaced the cutter and I am in the photo again. I was never keen to be in photos, but Mum insisted. She said I might like to look back at them one day. Mums always know best.

Lucky Seven served him more than 30 years, and only once did boat number eight come into contention. For that, *The Curse of the Westerly Wind* can be blamed yet again.

Pop was not there when that westerly struck, smashing the mooring and setting Lucky Seven free. The boat was swept out to sea. Everyone assumed it would swamp in the middle of the gulf, and sink. But two weeks later, it washed up near the Semaphore Jetty, having crossed the gulf and come ashore only a mile from the family home. It was undamaged, with barely a drop of water in it. Pop cancelled an order he had placed for a fibreglass boat that would have been its inferior replacement. It was something he was more than happy to do.

Lucky Seven was a 16-foot, carvel planked, open dinghy. Pop had it fitted with a 5-horsepower, Simplex, 4-stroke motor; the same as had powered our much bigger cutter. He was making sure that no sea would ever send this boat backwards.

Pop's new boat was not as pretty as the Clausen, but well designed for its purpose. Its hull had generous freeboard and was nicely rounded at the water line. We could carelessly turn Lucky Seven beam-on in the biggest sea without fear of a mishap, and there was never a danger of taking a wave over the stern. Only the bow could be criticized, for it was finer than on most boats. Taking a huge wave head on in the cutter, would see the cutter stop dead in the water. Taking the same wave on in the Clausen, would have the Clausen stand almost upright on its transom, then slam down hard, throwing spray to both sides. Lucky Seven would slice through such waves like a battle ship, but the spray would come over the bow and drench the crew.

I recall the occasion I took Lloyd out in Lucky Seven. Lloyd seldom went out, for he could not manage the soft tidal flat, due to his disability. On this day, he made a special effort, for he was keen to give his expert opinion on Pop's new boat. This meant crossing the flats, as the boat was anchored just beyond the outer reef. While negotiating the soft ground, Lloyd fell face first in the mud – several times. On each occasion, he vented the most amazing language skyward, to whom I could only guess. It reminded me of one of Lloyd's own stories. One about a ketch captain who would climb the rigging during a storm, shake his fist at the sky, then shout, "Come down here and fight me like a man." I think Forest Gump witnessed a similar performance.

Undeterred by his soaked condition, Lloyd went fishing. We fished for several hours, all the time the sea breeze getting stronger and the waves bigger. It was late in the day when an almost dry Lloyd became soaked once more, this time by spray coming over the bow. Specialised waterproof clothing was unknown at that time. Army coats and flimsy raincoats served as our waterproof garments. To deal with spray, we held a chaff bag up as a shield, but Lloyd could not hold up a bag and hang on at the same time. He told me in no uncertain terms, that he considered Pop's new boat to be the worst sea-boat he had ever been in. This upset me a little.

"How many boats can do this?" I snorted, as I swung the boat beam on to the sea.

Lloyd panicked, expecting the next wave to either roll us or swamp us. He shouted unflattering remarks in my direction, but they were too late. The next wave was already upon us. Lucky Seven lifted, tilted slightly, and the wave passed harmlessly beneath. I continued beam on until Lloyd was satisfied that we were in no danger. Next, I turned and ran the boat with the waves. Lucky Seven surfed beautifully, with no tendency to breach. Lloyd revised his opinion and gave the vessel his approval.

With Frank's departure, Mum and I became the permanent members of the crew, though Mum's bad back restricted her to calmer days. My crewman's share of the catch was the proceeds from the sale of squid, Red Mullet and sharks. It was good pocket money for a kid in high school, but not reliable. I caught my squid in the slack tide, when Whiting took a rest from biting. On days when Pop moved between grounds during slack water, my takings were poor.

Transportation was another issue that needed to be addressed when Frank departed, for Frank's ute was our only means of transport. Pop had to buy a car. When this had been asked of him seven years earlier, he had no money. Hence, Frank had been the one who had always provided the motor vehicle. But Pop had caught a lot of fish since then. This time, he was able to go into the car showroom closest his office in the city and choose a brand new, Holden Special, in two-tone grey. After that, he ordered a trailer, painted grey to match the car.

33 ROBBIE ASKS A FAVOUR

A lot changed in 1959, all the result of Black Point being opened up for shack development. The pending invasion of newcomers convinced two of Black Point's existing residents to leave. Robbie and Doc both moved to Pine Point, as we had done three years earlier. They bought freehold land on Billy Goat Flat and built permanent dwellings for themselves. It seemed that Pop and Robbie were destined to never be far apart. In fact, they were becoming quite good friends.

Robbie erected a chill-room alongside his new residence and offered Pop the use of it. The chill-room would save Pop the trouble of storing his fish on ice. Pop declined the offer, as he did not want others to see what he was catching. He was fishing places no one else fished, and people might follow him if they knew the success he was having.

However, Pop did take advantage of Robbie's chill-room to store his Razor Fish. Pop used Razor Fish for ground bait and went through two chaff bags a day. Razor Fish are large molluscs, and Pop gathered them in our bay at low tide. Eventually, he wiped the bay clear of Razor Fish, and it took 20 years for them to re-establish, once he gave up fishing. Pop would crush the Razor Fish and throw them over the back of the boat to attract the fish.

There were several others who also used Robbie's chill-room. Most notable was Rex Tyrrell, who we first met on the southern grounds four years earlier. Rex was no longer fishing for Whiting. He had a new boat, specially designed for a new fishing venture. Made from fibreglass, it was deep blue in colour; a break from the normal tradition of a white hull. The boat was about 20 feet long and could plane across the water at speed. Each morning, Rex would disappear over the horizon, headed for the same area we had seen Robbie head for years earlier. Each afternoon, Rex would return with a large catch of Snapper. We guessed Robbie had told him the marks to his ancient shipwreck, and Rex and he were in partnership.

In 1983, our suspicion was all but confirmed, when a wreck was discovered in the area where Robbie and Rex both fished. I read an article telling how Rex Tyrrell, a retired fisherman, had taken authorities to a hitherto unknown shipwreck. Divers identified the wreck to be that of the Zanoni.

The Zanoni was a 338-ton, three-masted, sailing ship. On the 11th February 1867, she set sail out of Port Wakefield. The weather was calm that morning, and the captain made course for Port Adelaide, from where the ship would sail on to London. However, early that afternoon, a storm approached from the west and unleashed a burst of fury that rolled the ship over. She sank within minutes, but fortunately, all 16 on board made it to the lifeboats.

The Zanoni had fallen victim to *The Curse of the Westerly Wind.* She would lay in 60 feet of water, officially missing for the next 116 years. Today, her final resting place is a protected historical site, as the Zanoni is one of Australia's best-preserved shipwrecks. Fishing is banned within 550 metres of where she lies.

It was not long after Pop began using the chill-room, that Robbie called in the favour. Robbie told us about his wife living in their house at Port Adelaide. Rita was her name, and she worked in the city. Their house was a ten-minute walk from where we lived at Largs Bay and four doors down from my music teacher. This last bit of information amazed me, for I had never seen Robbie's distinctive truck parked at the house.

Robbie explained how a lack of suitable transport made it difficult for Rita to get to Pine Point, and they wanted to always be together on weekends. Rita had tried coming over on the bus but found the trip too tiring. A car was her only option, but she could not drive. Robbie asked if we could help. We came every weekend and Pop's new car had three spare seats. We also lived close to their Port Adelaide home. Robbie thought that Rita could make good use of one of our spare seats.

We wondered how it was we knew nothing of Rita, or Robbie's house being so close. But nothing about Robbie ever came as a complete surprise. It was picturing him as a married man that was difficult. We knew the mad man persona was an act. We knew he had a heart of gold. It was just difficult to imagine Robbie the Romantic.

Pop was happy to oblige Robbie's request, and we found Rita to be pleasant company. She was our regular passenger for the next six years and would mostly nod off for the journey. We would wake her on arrival, and Robbie was always excited to see her. They were a devoted couple, and doted on each other. Rough old Robbie had his romantic side.

34 TWO INCHES FROM DISASTER

If I were to sum the memorable moments of my life, they would total mere seconds, and I think this applies to most of us. I had such a moment on Lucky Seven, not long after Pop launched it. What happened was over in an instant, but has left an image that will stay with me forever.

I was 14 years old and had just taken over Frank's position in Pop's fishing crew. We were fishing the Harvester, and I had just hooked the first Snapper for the evening. It was a 15-pounder, and I was making easy work of it on my hand-line. As always, I was using two hooks, and the fish was on the bottom hook. I prepared to land my catch, flicking the top hook into the boat, where it hung against my leg. I twisted the line through my fingers to get the firm grip needed to lift the fish. It was then that my foot slipped and I fell forward, teetering over the gunwale. The fish grasped the opportunity and turned. The balance of the battle was now in its favour. I did not have the adult strength to hold it, and was in danger of being pulled over the side if I did not let go of the line. But, I could not let go either, for the top hook was somewhere behind me. If I did, the next day's newspaper might read, *Boy fisherman disappears overboard after being hooked by a fish*. I did not wish to feature in a story where fish and fisherman reversed roles.

Quickly, I moved to avoid the missing boy outcome, and wrapped my left arm over the gunwale, my right shoulder now touching the water. A tug of war followed, and I was stretched to the limit. I hung on, slowly turning the fish's head back toward the boat.

Pop was anxious to see the fish on board, and became somewhat bemused to see so much of me hanging over the side. "What do you think you are doing?" he asked in a tone that suggested I should stop messing around.

"Sorry Pop, my foot slipped," I explained, looking at him and taking my eyes off the water. That was the instant I felt the fish go. "Lost him," I exclaimed in the same breath. Pop was not happy.

"How many times have I told you that if you lose a fish you lose the school," he scolded.

I pulled my hand out of the water to inspect the hook from which the fish had just escaped. Spitting the hook was the only way a fish could escape, for no Snapper could break a 200-pound line. There was no hook, just two inches of line protruding from my clenched fist. I looked back to where I last saw the fish. That was the memorable moment.

"No, *he* took it," I gasped.

There, just below my arm, close enough to touch, was the head of a 16-foot White Pointer shark. It was in the process of rolling its massive body. Moments earlier, it must have been belly up, just below the surface. My Snapper had almost certainly gone down its throat, and it had chomped its jaws so close to my hand. The length of line protruding from my fingers told me exactly how close those teeth had come: two inches. It had all had happened at the end of my arm, and I had seen none of it.

The rest of the night was good. I had my hand, the shark went away, and the school stayed on. We had a good catch. On the way in, I suggested to Pop that I had lost a White Pointer, not a Snapper. I might only have had it on for a short while, but it was almost in the boat. That had to count for something.

Pop had little to say on the subject. My guess is that he was both pleased and relieved. Some of the good luck that had kept him safe all these years, appeared to have rubbed off on his son.

35 PORT LINCOLN TOM

In 1974, a book was published called *Jaws*. The reaction to this book fascinated me. It was as if the world had become aware of White Pointers for the first time. People began having nightmares about them. The world and I were suddenly on the same page. I had grown up with White Pointers featuring in my bad dreams. I dreamt of one shark in particular, Port Lincoln Tom. I would be looking out from the kitchen window and see him swimming in the back lawn, daring me to come out and play.

The Harvester was the province of White Pointer sharks. They would arrive in springtime, following the large schools of Snapper. Most were about 16 feet long, but Port Lincoln Tom was the exception. Tom was a very old shark, estimated to be about 22 feet long. Age had made him slow, and he had outlived the clean, White Pointer image, for he had yellow blotches on his underbelly.

White Pointers are the masters of the ocean. They swim with a slow arrogance, reluctant to show the flighty movements common to other sharks. You only see them if they wish to be seen. They hang back in the gloom, sizing you up. If you arouse their curiosity, they come into view. To see a White Pointer is to know he is interested in you. It is a very uneasy feeling.

Port Lincoln Tom was master of them all. It seemed an eternity whenever he swam by. A huge grey ghost that would suddenly appear from nowhere, and then disappear again. Frank once likened his dorsal fin to a toy yacht cruising past in the moonlight.

My bad dreams were derived from the graphic stories told by Pop and Frank. Others who had made Tom's acquaintance, readily supported their stories. Only once did I ever meet the great shark.

It was in 1959, and I had invited a friend from school to come Snapper fishing with us. This was a rarity, for Pop discouraged visitors, as he did not want people knowing how many fish we were catching. Somehow, my friend Yanis Ozlins, cleared Pop's security check. I suspected his academic achievement in class might have gained him favour. Pop may have been hoping that Yanis's zeal for study would somehow inspire me.

We took Yanis to the Harvester, but it proved to be a slow morning, for the Harvester failed to produce its usual catch of a dozen Snapper. Seldom did it produce less; some mornings it produced more. On this morning, it failed to produce anything.

Yanis was hanging over the side of the boat, blankly staring into the water. I was sitting on the other side, for there is always a need to keep things balanced in a small boat. Suddenly, Yanis yelled out, "What's that?"

Not wishing to unbalance things, I looked over my side, not expecting to see anything, for it was on his side, but I saw it too.

A huge black mass under the boat. I immediately thought of a stingray, but it was too big. Everything under the boat was black. I ran my eye outward, trying to determine an outline. It terminated in a point. I was looking at the right pectoral fin of a huge shark. Yanis was seeing the same thing, only he was seeing the left.

The shape moved on, then made a second pass about a minute later. This time, it was almost in touching distance. The brighter light closer to the surface revealed the body to be grey. First, we saw a head, with two small black eyes inspecting us. This inspection left no doubt that we were intruders, and could be dealt with any way this monster pleased. We continued watching, until finally, a huge tail passed. We looked again toward the head, trying to gauge the creature's full length, but the head was already lost in the dull water.

"Guess that's what's keeping the Snapper away," Pop grumbled. "Are you boys happy to stay here until he goes away, or would you rather we went off and tried for Whiting?" Pop was proud of the fact that no shark had ever driven him off a fishing ground.

"Whiting fishing sounds good," said Yanis, who appeared a little concerned about his current surroundings.

Reluctantly, Pop obliged our guest, and once we were on our way, Yanis had questions.

"That must be the biggest shark in the whole world," he pronounced.

Pop then explained, "South Australia's west coast has a shark they call Barnacle Lil. I think that shark holds the title. Our shark is called Port Lincoln Tom. I don't know how it got that name, but it's a boy's name. I guess Barnacle Lil is a girl, and not the same shark. Maybe Port Lincoln Tom is the second biggest shark in the world."

36 THE ROCK

Among the memories I treasure the most from Pop's Secret Fishing World, are the people who lived there. They were different to city folk, and always had time to talk to a kid like me. I found them more interesting, for they took pleasure from the simple things around them, and worried less about issues that occupied the thoughts of those back in Adelaide.

The Henderson brothers were among that interesting group of people. Charlie was the younger and more vibrant of the two brothers. When telling Charlie something of interest, he would most often respond with the words, *Goodness gracious me*. He was in his late seventies and had a liking for anything containing alcohol. The fact that Pine Point had no pub was the blessing that had kept him alive for so many years. The nearest pub was 10 miles away, in Ardrossan. The distance posed a significant barrier to someone who did not have a motor vehicle. However, Charlie did have a horse and cart, and on occasions, the old horse would take him on the journey.

They would arrive at Ardrossan, and Charlie would hitch the horse to a post outside the pub. The horse's job was to look after the cart. This would take all day, for having made the long journey, Charlie would be in no a hurry to return home. Close to dark, Charlie's drinking companions would carry him out and lay him in the cart. This done, they would light a hurricane lamp that hung from the back. This served as a tail light. The rest was up to the horse. He would set off down the road as darkness descended. Some hours later, Charlie would wake up in his backyard, still in the cart, his faithful old horse patiently waiting to be released from duty.

The older Henderson was Fred, a retired fisherman in his early eighties. He was our nearest Pine Point neighbour, though technically, he was not our neighbour. Fred and Charlie had houses on the same street, which was a five-minute walk from where we were. But Fred also had a shed on the beach, close to our boat shed.

Each morning, Fred would walk from home to his shed. There, he would sit on an upturned kerosene tin and blissfully stare out at his two fishing boats sitting on their moorings. Next to him would be Mick, his faithful Kelpie, whose scraggy appearance was similar to a famous Kelpie called Red Dog, who earned notoriety as the Pilbara Wanderer a decade later. Unlike Red Dog, Fred's Kelpie was a one-man dog, and had a special feature that distinguished him from all other dogs. Pop called it his badge of office - a badly scarred nose, legacy of Mick's renowned ability to successfully hunt crabs on the tidal flats.

Like Mick, Fred's appearance was a little unkempt. He was short in stature, and like Robbie, I believe was also a jockey in his younger days. An oversized white moustache covered much of his weathered face, and the same shabby hat was always on his balding head. Only his eyes defied their age. They twinkled whenever Fred spoke.

Fred's clothes were well washed, but he could do nothing about the permanent stains that gave them character. His baggy trousers stayed up courtesy of a length of rope tied around his waist. I suggested to Pop that we buy Fred a belt for Christmas, but Pop thought that would most likely offend. There was no doubt that Fred had the financial means to buy new clothes, but the Pine Point store did not sell clothes, and that was as far as Fred ever went.

At times, this feature of Fred's life would attract speculation. If he only went to the Pine Point store and that was where he cashed his pension cheque, what did he do with the money he did not spend? It must be somewhere.

Fred lived in a neat, timber-framed cottage, and was proud to show visitors his small living room. To him, it was a shrine to all the great racehorses; its timber panelled walls covered with pictures of racehorses that Fred had cut from magazines. Fred glued the pictures to the timber panels and varnished them over. He delighted in showing people his ornate walls. They were his prized possession.

When a person passes away, others usually value their prized possessions. We had known Fred for about three years when he passed away. I was walking along the Pine Point gully a short time later and found Fred's cherished racehorse pictures on the ground. The panelling from his living room walls had been ripped out and lay in a smashed up pile on the gully floor. I reported my find to Pop and suggested that Fred's house must have termites. "I suspect people have been looking for something other than termites," was Pop's reply.

It was in 1959 that Fred told Pop about the Rock, his old Snapper ground that had been known to only a few. Fred's marks for the Rock had been trees that were no longer there, but he told Pop approximately where the Rock was to be found. Stories about the Rock were well known in the district, including one about a ketch running onto it in the early 1900s, causing authorities to blast part of the Rock away. Given the depth of water Fred said the Rock was in, we considered this an unlikely story.

The Rock became something Pop had to find, but with so little to go on, it would be like looking for a needle in a haystack. Then an opportunity arose. It was a day when the fishing was slow. Pop and I were wondering what to do, when we noticed a boat well out to sea. Boats were uncommon in the area, and this one appeared to be where Fred had indicated we would find the Rock. As the fish had failed to inspire us where we were, we made full speed for the mystery boat. Full speed was walking pace. Boats were not fast in the fifties. As expected, the chase was useless, for the mystery boat moved off before we were close enough to see what it was doing. We concluded it was travelling up the gulf and had made a brief stop for no particular reason. However, we had nothing better to do, and so we continued on to the approximate area where the boat had been. As expected, we found the water too deep to see the bottom. I thought to myself, *What would Robbie do in this situation?*

I stared over the side, thinking I might see a large rock looming up from the seabed, but knowing that chance was slim. Pop was at the tiller. We began to circle. Suddenly, we motored over a school of Trevally about 10 feet below the surface. They were not ordinary Trevally. They were four-pounders. The only place we had seen

Trevally that size was on the Harvester. We went back and anchored over the school.

It was a significant moment. That was how Pop found his Rock, and never again did he go to the Harvester. The mystery boat that drew us to the area never returned, and for years, Pop fished the Rock, untroubled by other boats. Apart from being a ground far superior to the Harvester, not once did we ever encounter a White Pointer shark, though we often wondered if it was the Bronze Whalers that kept them away.

The Rock was a fish magnet, and Pop introduced a new species to his fishing vocabulary. *Pigs*.

I caught my first big Snapper when I was 9 years old. It would have weighed about 15 pounds - a midget compared to Pop's Pigs.

Pops Pigs were 30-pound Snapper that arrived at the Rock in September, two months earlier than the big schools at the Harvester. Their colouring was darker than normal Snapper, and on a good night Pop would stop fishing once he had all he could handle.

I never took part in one of Pop's big catches at the Rock. I called them Friday Night Fish. Pop's job gave him a degree of flexibility in how he worked his hours. On Fridays, when the Snapper were running at the Rock, Pop would leave work early and fish that evening.

Pop and Frank setting out from the boat shed for a night on the Snapper. Pop is carrying his trusty portable radio, which was never far from his side.

I would arrive well after dark, having skipped the last class at school in order to catch the only bus that went to Pine Point. On those nights, I would wait for Pop's return at low tide. He would bring the boat to the reef and on board would be more than a quarter of a ton of Snapper. They had to be cleaned, carried over the soft tidal flats, and iced down. And added to my Friday night chores, was the bad news that there would be no more fishing that weekend, because the iceboxes would be full.

Fish market boxes were not designed to hold Pop's 30-pound Pigs.

My paddleboard was put into service on such nights. The paddleboard was our multipurpose marine vessel. I used it as a tender when the tide was too high for comfortable wading to Pop's boat. It was my second attempt to build a tender, not wishing to swim with another Bronze Whaler as I had done three years earlier while retrieving the Clausen. My first attempt had been a six-foot canvas paddleboat. I used timber salvaged from Ron and Glad's wrecked dinghy for its frame. The paddleboat served for two years, then one night, a high tide swept it off the beach and smashed it on the rocks at the end of the bay.

My first boat. This is me at age 13, sitting in the canvas boat I made from timber we salvaged from Ron and Glad's wrecked dingy. It served as the tender to Pop's boat until it got washed off the beach one night and was wrecked.

The paddleboard was simple in design, being eight feet long, two feet wide, and six inches at its deepest point. It had a timber frame encased in a bondwood skin. Pop bought the materials and trusted me not to make a mess of the job. It was my first major woodworking project. I was 14 years old and keen to prove that I could do the things my big brother could do. Happily, the paddleboard floated, though it always leaked a little.

On Snapper nights, the paddleboard became a sled with a rope tied to the front for towing. We would pile it with Snapper, and then drag it across the tidal flat, sliding over the soft ground and through the pools of water. It took several trips to bring in all the fish.

Pop had no way of knowing that there was no large rock on the ground he called the Rock, as he had no sonar to tell him what was under his boat. Pop was fishing on a reef, one of several in the area. For some reason, which we had yet to understand, the fish considered this reef special. The Rock was, in fact, some distance away.

Local landowner, Ron Harvey, regularly fished what I believe was the rock Fred told us about. Ron and Pop had a gentleman's agreement. They never went near each other's grounds. Ron was also part of the small group who knew about the Harvester ground at the time Pop and Frank first fished there, for I am told it was Ron's harvester that was sitting on the reef. However, I cannot recall Ron ever fishing the Harvester. He preferred his Rock.

Ron was one of Pine Point's characters. He was a landowner of means, but could easily be mistaken for being a fisherman or farm labourer. I recall a time when Ron bought a new car. Some considered the transportation of live sheep on the back seat of the latest model Jaguar, to be sacrilege. Ron's comment was, "A car is no good to a farmer if he can't throw a couple of sheep in the back from time to time."

Ron had a son, John, who was more interested in moving pictures than farming or fishing. He managed the Maitland Picture Theatre, some 24 miles from Pine Point. Ron decided that Pine Point should have its own picture theatre. He knew the town was too small for such an establishment, but thought it might attract an audience at holiday time. Ron built a theatre on the vacant land next to his house, with John as manager. The building still stands but the last picture show was many years ago.

In later years, long after Ron had stopped fishing, I went looking for his fishing spot. Equipped with sonar, I found a rock. I was disappointed. Unlike Pop's reef, it is not a fish magnet.

37   THE STORY OF PENGWEE

Our little bay played host to most of the fish and bird species that were to be found along the coast. Occasionally, however, there would be the unusual visitor. One of these was a freshwater Trout caught by Trevor Hay, a friend about my age. Trevor netted the fish not far from our boat shed, but we all had difficulty believing that it was a Trout as there are no freshwater streams on Yorke Peninsula. Trevor took it to the Adelaide Museum, where a marine expert confirmed it to be a Brown Trout. The expert's theory was that it had swum from the Little Para River on the other side of the gulf.

The trout was unusual, but we had another visitor that also caused a degree of disbelief. For me, that story began shortly after I hitched Pop's boat to the mooring. I was wading the last 20 yards to shore, when a little black head began to circle in the water. It was like a puppy looking for a friend to give it a pat. I ignored it, for I was tired from a long day's fishing. It was only as I walked up the beach that it occurred to me, it was not a head I recognised, but I did not go back to investigate.

There were other people on the beach that afternoon, for the blocks surveyed at the same time as ours, now all had shacks. One belonged to a family of four from Elizabeth, a newly developed satellite suburb north of Adelaide. The dad was English, and the mum, French. They had two kids who were about my age, a boy Jeanpierre, and a girl Cathie (or perhaps Kathie). They also had two well-groomed French Poodles.

The kids and the poodles were playing on the beach when the little black head swam up to them. It tried to come out of the water, but the dogs chased it back. It was a small Fairy Penguin, a bird not resident in the gulf. The nearest colony was about 80 miles south, on Kangaroo Island.

The kids took the dogs away and tied them up, then returned to the beach. The penguin came out of the water and waddled up to them, showing no fear. It had a large gash from head to tail, running diagonally down its back. How it had survived such a wound was a mystery. The kids guessed it had been struck by a boat propeller.

The little bird appeared to want company, and apparently, the kids looked like good companionship material. It followed them around the beach. They ran up to the shack and the penguin followed. The penguin met their parents.

"Can we keep it, can we keep it?" the kids pestered.

The answer was, "No."

Though unhappy with the decision, the kids led the bird back in the water and untied the dogs. The penguin swam away and they thought that was the last they would see of it. Next morning, they got up early. The dogs had been inside all night, which meant the penguin might still be on the beach. They rushed out but did not go far, for the penguin was standing on their doorstep. It had probably been there all night, and its persistence paid off, for their parents could resist no longer. The kids were allowed take the bird home, but only until it was nursed back to good health.

What happened next was something I first read about in the newspaper. There was a photo of the kids and the penguin, and the penguin had been given a name, Pengwee.

Elizabeth was Adelaide's most inland suburb. It was also Adelaide's hottest, and much of it open paddocks. To this day, I muse when I think of the man living down the street from the kids. It was during a hot spell, and the man was watering his front lawn. At the appropriate time, he went out to move the sprinkler, and there standing under it, was a penguin. The man thought penguins only lived at the South Pole.

I would have loved to have been there when he rushed inside to explain the situation to his wife. Once she confirmed that the heat had not made him delusional, they rang the newspaper, the police, and anyone else they could think of. Everyone confirmed what the man was finding hard to believe. It was a penguin.

Authorities soon traced the bird back to the kids, and decided that it was in good hands. Pengwee returned to the kid's makeshift hospital where it received a lecture on the perils of escaping. The kids then continued with their tender loving care. Shortly thereafter, the patient was ready to be discharged, but the only penguin colony within reach of Adelaide, was on Granite Island, near Victor Harbor.

Pengwee was packed into a cardboard box and driven to Victor Harbor, a two-hour drive from Elizabeth. On arrival, the family marched across the causeway to Granite Island, the kids taking turns to gently carry the box with its precious passenger.

Alas, disappointment waited for them on the island. There were no penguins. They sat down close to the water's edge, pondering what to do. All the time, Pengwee was becoming more and more restless in the box. Finally, they decided to let their little friend out, for they could not make a life for it in Elizabeth, and Pine Point was certainly not its home.

Pengwee surprised them all. They expected to see their little penguin dive into the sea and swim off to find friends. Instead, it rushed up the hill behind them, and disappeared. The family followed and found burrows. They looked inside, and in each, they saw little sets of penguin eyes, looking out at them. Pengwee had found a home.

38 DRAMA NIGHT

There was one shark story the family has told more than any other, the reason being, Mum was closest to the action. I was there too, and Mum often called on me to be her witness. When telling the story, she usually left out the things that she had to say to Pop and me. Her words were out of character and not at all complimentary.

It promised to be a perfect Snapper night. The air was warm, the sea calm, the tide right, and the Snapper were running. Pop convinced Mum to come fishing with us. Mum had never fished for Snapper at night, but this was her night to try.

We arrived at the Rock on dusk, and the fish did not let us down. So hungry were the Snapper, that 10-pounders ripped the line through our fingers before the bait reached the bottom. Pop declared conditions the same as the time he caught 106 Snapper on the Harvester. It was all about to happen again.

Unfortunately, it did not happen again, for we never saw those fish that ran the line through our fingers. A pack of Bronze Whalers moved in. When pulling in a Snapper, we always wanted the fish pulling away from us. If a fish made a rush to the surface, it meant a shark was in pursuit. These fish all rushed to the surface, a short-lived rush; for a sudden thump on the line would tell us that the fish was no more. Sharks took fish after fish. Pop was frustrated, but he persisted, hoping that the sharks would eventually eat their fill and go away.

"If we fill 'em up with fish, they will go away," Pop declared.

At that moment, there were simultaneous splashes on both sides of the boat. Mum was horrified. She was surrounded by sharks.

"Don't be stupid," she yelled. "You don't even know how many sharks there are."

Pop had to prove to Mum that his plan would work. He hooked a Snapper, then using every ounce of strength, pulled it in as quickly as possible. He saw his fish almost to the boat, when a shark rushed from the side and bit it in two. Pop continued pulling, lifting the remaining half, high out of the water.

"Look," he said, thinking he could prove a point to Mum. "This time they have left me the head."

At that moment, a shark came out of the water like a dolphin at Sea World, and Pop no longer had the head. Mum saw firsthand, a shark's ability to see things above the water, even at night. She was not impressed.

Pop baited up again, and I am not sure what happened next, for I was looking away. What I do recall was Mum rushing past me toward the bow, and Pop stepping back toward the engine box. They were attempting to counterbalance an eight-foot shark writhing on the back deck. Its head was where Pop had moments before been standing. Fortunately, Pop stopped the shark coming further into the boat, and after several seconds, managed to push it back into the water.

Mum's disapproval became louder, but Pop just cursed his luck. Not wishing to give up, he tried a different strategy. He guessed that the Snapper were just under the boat. He baited with a squid head, and let out a mere 10 feet of line. The plan was to hook a fish close to the boat, and get it in before a shark had a chance to grab it. It was a bad plan, because Bronze Whalers like squid heads.

Pop hooked a ten-foot Bronze Whaler, and the 200-pound breaking strain line brought the shark to a halt. It was tethered, 10 feet below the boat. The shark began to swim in frantic circles. Phosphorous stirred by its pounding tail, created a spectacular, underwater, fireworks display.

Finally, the shark realised that going in a circle was getting it nowhere. It made a mad rush for the surface and stood on its tail, so close to Mum that she could have reached out and touched it. Mum was certain that the shark was going to come down on top of her, and we were thinking much the same. Fortunately, it fell like a giant log, alongside the boat, breaking the line and splashing us all in the process.

When Pop Took Us Fishing

Pop immediately set about looking for another hook. That shark was just another setback in what promised to be a good night's fishing. When Mum realised his intent, she took charge, expressing her alternate plan.

"We are going in," she declared.

At this point in the story, I must explain that Mum was not one for drama. She could remain calm in a crisis. I recall an evening three years later, when a large scorpion wandered in while she was cooking tea. None of us noticed our little guest arrive until Mum accidentally trod on it. A very upset scorpion stung Mum on her bare foot.

Mum screamed, causing Pop to look up from the TV. "What's wrong?"

"That thing bit me." Mum was looking down, pointing at the scorpion.

Pop quickly came to Mum's rescue. The intruder was no match for his slipper. Moments later, its corpse was thrown out the door.

Mum looked worried. "Scorpions are poisonous aren't they?"

Pop's voice was calm and assuring. "I don't think anyone has ever died from a scorpion bite."

"But it really stings," Mum insisted.

"Don't worry, the stinging will go away." Pop's tone suggested that he was a scorpion expert, but I doubt this was the case. Mum went on cooking and the stinging must have subsided, because she failed to mention it again.

But on this infamous Snapper night, Mum was not convinced that Pop was thinking rationally. He was at his risk taking best. She could see that the sharks were not going away, and Pop's assurances otherwise, held little value.

Mum looked to me for support, and I said I had always trusted Pop's judgement where sharks were concerned. That was it. She declared us both nuts, and if anyone had been standing on the shore that night, they might have heard her words floating across the water. Pop gave in. I think he realised he had more to fear from Mum than the sharks. I carefully pulled up the anchor, not wanting it to be attacked by the sharks that were "monstering" everything that moved.

Mum often told this story, and Pop cautioned me not to elaborate on it. Pop always played down the shark danger to Mum, and was relieved that it was the last shark that had impressed her the most. I was never to mention how Lucky Seven proved its worth that night. Had we been in the Clausen, the shark on the back would have sunk us for sure.

39 SNAPPER TAKE A DIVE

1962 was the year I finally shook off the shackles of school and joined the workforce. I started as the office boy for Austral Sheet Metal Works Limited, a company that made everything from teapots to wine vats. As expected, work proved to be far more fun than school, and my duties included four mail runs a day. I maintained the flow of paper throughout the factory and office, as well as going to the post office on the company bicycle. I told people that I was the most important person on staff, and if it were not for me, everything would come to a halt. No one shared my view, but important or not, my job was freedom, and at the end of the week, I got paid.

At night, I studied accountancy through the Hemmingway and Robertson Institute, and again, as expected, I found it dull. But Pop said I would never be out of a job once qualified, and I could see the logic in that. On weekends, I fished at Pine Point. All this left no time for sport or a normal teenage social life. I figured they could come later when I was no longer a teenager.

A lot of changes were happening around that time. The scramble for weekend shacks was occurring everywhere. Black Point beach was filling fast, and more weekend fishermen were appearing all the time. The newcomers soon found Harvester and many of the Whiting grounds, but Pop's Rock remained beyond their reach, and Snapper at the Rock was his main interest. Then, an alarming development occurred at a place called Cape Jervis, south of Adelaide. Fishermen were building shacks there too. They were 80 miles distant by sea from Pine Point, but their activities gave Pop a big problem.

The currents around the cape are very fast, but once a fortnight, a dodge tide slows the current for about three days. Fishermen at the cape discovered that vast quantities of Snapper could be taken during the dodge tide period. In the weeks leading up to Christmas, their catches would flood the market, causing the price for Snapper to crash to almost give-away status. There were stories of Snapper going to the dump. They were no longer worth catching. By contrast, the price of Whiting rose to record levels in the run up to Christmas. Somehow, Robbie seemed to know all this was going to happen, and had already given up fishing for Snapper. He was now an inshore net fisherman.

Pop decided our future lay in Whiting, but for this, he needed new grounds that he did not have to share. The water north of Pine Point was too deep for Whiting, and everyone was now fishing around Black Point. All that was left, was Robbie's southern grounds beyond Black Point, but they were too far away. We only went to the southern grounds in February, when the fish gathered at the Big Hole. Robbie had told us there were more Whiting on the southern grounds than we could imagine, but we had never found that many.

The drop in the Snapper price also effected Frank. He gave up fishing for them and asked Pop if he wished to take back the Clausen. Like most of my friends, I was saving for my first car, but the Clausen changed all that. I used my savings to buy my first boat; the car would have to wait. The Clausen returned to its old home in the boat shed.

1962 was also the year my parents purchased freehold land on Billy Goat Flat. They built a small dwelling that became their preferred residence for much of their retirement. I saw an irony in this. The effort to buy Mum's dream house had resulted in them having a second more humble home, which they preferred. I became caretaker, and for most times sole resident, of Mum's dream house back in Largs Bay.

Mum was happy in her little Pine Point home. It had all the luxuries the boat shed lacked. It had mains water, electricity, a flushing toilet, and even a bath. At last, she did not have to contend with snakes, spiders, and flies. But she missed one thing. She missed waking up to the sound of waves lapping on the beach, and warm morning sun streaming in through the screen wire door.

40 BILL MAGOR

The Pine Point Whiting grounds were the province of several fishermen, most notable being Bill Magor. Bill was tall and slim, his boat no bigger than the dinghy we once salvaged from the Port Canal. This combination of tall man and small boat would at times, produce an interesting optical illusion. Bill would stand whilst fishing, and he was all you could see. No boat, just a tall man standing on the water.

Bill had a friendly disposition and enjoyed a good chat. Whenever our boats were close, he would update us on local news. We got similar updates whenever we ran into him at the store, or around at Robbie's chill-room. But Bill was a good fisherman and maintained the Fisherman's Code of Secrecy. He never had interesting things to say about the fishing.

Each morning, we both fished the same ground, and I would watch Bill follow the Whiting up and down the reef. He used oars, for he did not want to disturb the fish with his motor. Mostly, he would only row a few yards before anchoring again. It was the same as I had watched Rex Tyrrell do four years earlier, only Bill would often double back over the same ground. Rex did not. Once Rex reached the end of Rex's Run, he would leave the area altogether. Bill was fishing on a reef bounded by tape weed. Rex's Run was on a huge reef system that went for almost a mile. I guessed that Whiting followed different rules in different places.

We had a lot to learn about Whiting, and could only learn by watching others. Finally, we did discover something for ourselves. Each morning, we would all race to the ground, for the boat that found the fish first, usually finished with the best catch. The reef was about 100 yards long, and the fish could be anywhere along it. We worked out that the direction of the wind dictated where we would find the fish. With this rule, we often got to the fish first. We later tried the rule in other places, but found nowhere else where it worked the same.

Another thing we learned by watching Bill, was the value of his glass bottom bucket. He used it to view the bottom. Bill would anchor, throw in ground bait, and then use his viewer to watch it settle. If no Whiting appeared, he did not bother to fish. He would row to the next spot. Even when catching fish, he would check from time to time to see what the fish were doing. This gave him clues as to where to go next, or if the fish had had enough, and it was time for him to leave. In those days, you were considered a poor fisherman if you fished a spot until the fish stopped biting. It was believed that this would teach fish to recognise the danger signs associated with fishermen and become more wary.

The final thing I copied from Bill was his fishing gear. Bill used a three-foot rod with low mounted overhead-geared reel, 25-pound line, and a 2-ounce sinker. Once I mastered the unusual technique needed for this setup, I regularly out-fished Pop, who always used a hand-line.

41 A FINAL FAREWELL

Once I had my own boat, it was necessary for me to have a commercial fishing licence. These were readily available and I think I paid five shillings, but I am not sure. However, I do have a memento that gives a clue on the value of licences in those days. I kept the tax return from my final year of commercial fishing. An item on it reads, *Licences $8.* This is far different to today's valuation. Fishing licences are now stringently controlled, and if that same unrestricted licence were to be available today, it would cost in excess of $100,000 to buy.

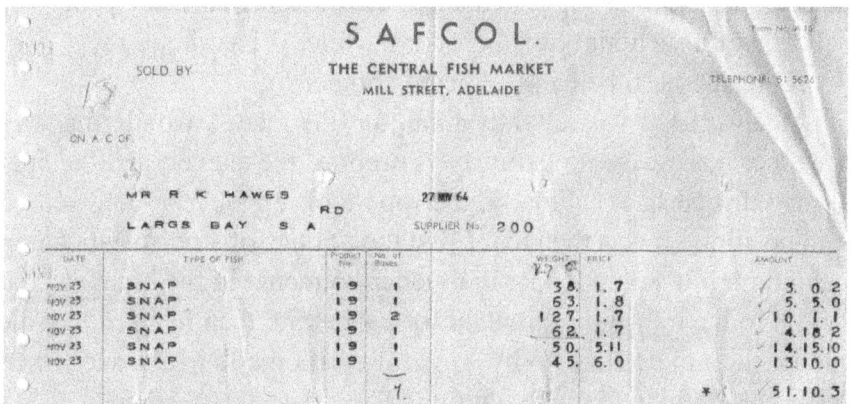

By the time I took up my commercial licence, our Snapper fishing had almost come to an end. I think I kept this 1964 account as a memento of one of the few Snapper catches that I put into the market. The account also appears to have a coding error as the prices for the bottom two lines suggest they were Whiting, not Snapper.

My first project as a licenced fisherman was to find new Whiting drops for Pop. Robbie had long sparked my interest in finding grounds, and I knew of many places where fishermen had never looked. Pop set me the task of exploring the southern grounds, where Robbie had promised we would find more Whiting than we could ever imagine. Boats often ventured to the southern grounds, but the vastness of the reef always defeated them. Most soon gave up looking, but I was determined to persevere until I knew every square inch of the place.

It was during an early excursion to the southern grounds that I had my final encounter with a White Pointer. By 1963, we had all but stopped fishing for Snapper, and I thought we had seen the last of big sharks. However, Pop gave me an extra task this day. Robbie had told him that people were catching Whiting on the Harvester and Pop asked me to check the ground on my journey south.

I arrived at the Harvester mid-morning and found a collection of boats already there. They were close together, about 40 yards from the harvester itself. None were catching fish, but the occupants were talking in tones that suggested a degree of excitement.

"Haven't seen him over here for a while," I heard one say.

"I'm sure he'll be back," I heard another.

Meanwhile, I was intently lining up the marks, wondering why the other boats were so far away. I dropped the anchor, and the boat slowly drifted back. Finally, the rope took up and the boat settled into position. It was then that I first took notice of a noise happening behind me. It sounded like the rudder bouncing in the brackets that held it to the transom. I thought for a moment, then realised that the rudder did not do that. Why would it do it on a flat calm day when there was nothing to make it move?

I took one last satisfied look at the marks and then turned to investigate the mystery noise. The rudder was bouncing up and down, just as I thought, but fortunately, not high enough to pop off the back. My eye then moved to a point, 18 feet beyond. A tail was gently swaying back and forth on the surface, holding its massive owner in the current. The near end of the creature was nudging the rudder with its nose. That was the only time a White Pointer ever made contact with my boat, but somehow, it did not bother me.

I went to the stern and leaned out over the transom. The shark was about 16 feet long.

Are you the bloke who nearly got my hand? I wondered.

The water was calm, and we made perfect eye contact. The shark stopped bouncing the rudder, like a naughty schoolboy that had been caught doing something he shouldn't. It was as if he had been trying to get my attention.

For several seconds, we just stared at each other, me wondering what the shark would do next. He was close to the surface, the Clausen blocking his way forward. Then he answered my question. He rolled on his side and a huge pectoral fin rose high out of the water. I remained leaning over the back. There was less than three-feet between us. The tip of the pectoral fin was level with my head. Then the monster arched his great body, and slid gently by, downward, under the boat. The last thing I saw as I peered below was a massive tail waving back at me. Then that too was gone. The encounter happened more than 50 years ago. I have not come across a White Pointer in the gulf since.

We always found White Pointers to be a predictable shark. They were solitary hunters that would inspect the boat, take one or two easy Snapper that they might find on our hand-lines, then move on. We assumed of course, that if you swam with one, you risked becoming a meal. I guess the fact that they had plenty of Snapper to eat, made them less dangerous.

I know White Pointers still roam the gulf, but I suspect, not as many. In recent times, I have heard stories of White Pointers biting propellers, boats, and even anchors. This was not our experience. These reports suggest that the current generation of shark is angrier. Perhaps they are hungrier because there is less food. Perhaps the abundance of boats has made them less wary, or perhaps some people tease them for amusement. The current practice of fixing berley munchers to the transom is definitely not a good idea.

Robbie had some thoughts on the danger of sharks. He once warned us not to paint the underside of our hull white, as he believed this would encourage sharks to attack the boat. I suspect Robbie gave Rex Tyrrell the same warning, because his boat which was purpose built to fish the Zanoni, had a blue hull. Today, most hulls are white all over, including mine.

Robbie also told a story about the time he chrome plated a single blade on his propeller. The theory was that the propeller would flash as he trolled for Snook, and the flashing would draw the Snook up from the weed bed. He soon gave up the idea, however, because a shark attacked his propeller. Today, many boats have shiny, stainless steel propellers.

42 THE SOUTHERN GROUNDS

My plan to explore the southern grounds was simple. I would cover the reef, a section at a time. First, I drew an imaginary triangle between the Big Hole, the Neck, and Rex's Run. This gave me a large area of reef from where to begin. Over the first season, I searched the area thoroughly, and found nothing. To my human eye, much of the area within the triangle looked more appealing to a fish than Rex's Run itself, but Rex's Run was where the fish chose to be. It was a mystery, and the reason why others had also been defeated. It meant I would have to check every bit of reef, not just places I thought looked likely.

Finally, a breakthrough came in circumstances not anticipated. My voyages south were mostly solo, but on this day, Pop and I were fishing together. On the previous weekend, I had found a good number of fish on the Big Hole, hence Pop's decision to join me. Our session was going well, when a boat appeared in the distance, headed straight for us. As the Big Hole was a place known only to us, Pop was not keen to share its secret with another. We moved well away, keeping one mark to the Big Hole, in line. This way, we could tell how close the nuisance boat would get to where the fish were.

The other boat anchored a good distance from the Big Hole, and we guessed they caught nothing, for it soon went away. Our fortunes were a little different. Whilst waiting for the boat to go, we put our lines over the side and began catching Whiting. We were in a place well outside my area of search. I was both happy and disappointed. After all my methodical searching, we find a spot by dumb luck. Pop named the drop the Goat's Horn.

In the year that followed, other boats discovered Rex's Run, which was no surprise. We knew it was only a matter of time, as Rex's Run went for some distance. Fortunately, Rex's Run was far enough away from the Big Hole and Goat's Horn, for the other boats not to bother us. From then on, we kept away from Rex's Run, leaving the other boats to fish it. We had plenty to keep us busy where we were.

Then, an interesting development occurred. The new boats found a drop where I had never looked. Again, I was disappointed. My exploration was yielding nothing, yet two new drops had been found since I had started looking. Was it bad luck, or simply that I had no idea what I was doing? According to Robbie, there were more Whiting on the southern grounds than we could imagine, but I had no results to show Pop. An unimaginable quantity of Whiting should have been easy to find. I wondered if Robbie had exaggerated his story, but then I recalled other things he had told me many years before.

Robbie appeared to place some significance on lines that join fishing drops, but when I had asked him if fish needed these lines so as not to become lost, he avoided the question. I decided to explore along the lines that joined the four main drops we knew. I had success and found a new drop that Pop christened the Bush. The Bush went on to become one of Pop's all-time top Whiting drops and other fishermen never found it.

The discovery of the Bush encouraged me to continue my search, and I followed the lines again, this time to see where they might take me to next. I used the distances between our known drops as a guide on how far I should go. Years earlier, Robbie had told me that distance was important when looking for fishing drops. At the time, he had been talking about Snapper grounds that were miles apart, but I wondered if his reasoning could be applied on a smaller scale.

In almost no time, I found four more drops. My searching had more than doubled the number of drops we had on the southern grounds, and they were widely scattered. It was then that I first began to wonder about something odd. I mapped the drops on paper. They formed a pattern. *Was the pattern coincidence, or part of nature's plan? Did Whiting drops have to bear a relationship to each other, and if so, why?* The pattern suggested where next I should try. I tried the places suggested by the pattern, but found no more fish. I concluded that the pattern was interesting, but my finds had been the result of persistence and good luck.

With so many new places to fish, Pop was keen to go south as often as possible. In 1964, I sold the Clausen and bought a 14-foot Bellboy fibreglass boat, powered by a 35-horsepower, Mercury outboard motor.

My third boat. Pop and I are about to launch my fibreglass boat from the beach in front of the boat shed. Its speed enabled us to get to the southern grounds far quicker than by going by Lucky Seven.

This solved the problem of distance, as it got us to the southern grounds much quicker. In good weather, we would go the shortest route possible; in rough weather, we hugged the coast.

Our routine from then on was to fish the Pine Point grounds in the morning, Mum and Pop in Lucky Seven, and me in my new, fibreglass boat. Between the two boats, we would average 10 dozen Whiting. Later that day, after most other boats had gone in, Pop and I would head south in my boat. In the last two hours of daylight, we would catch a further 20 dozen Whiting.

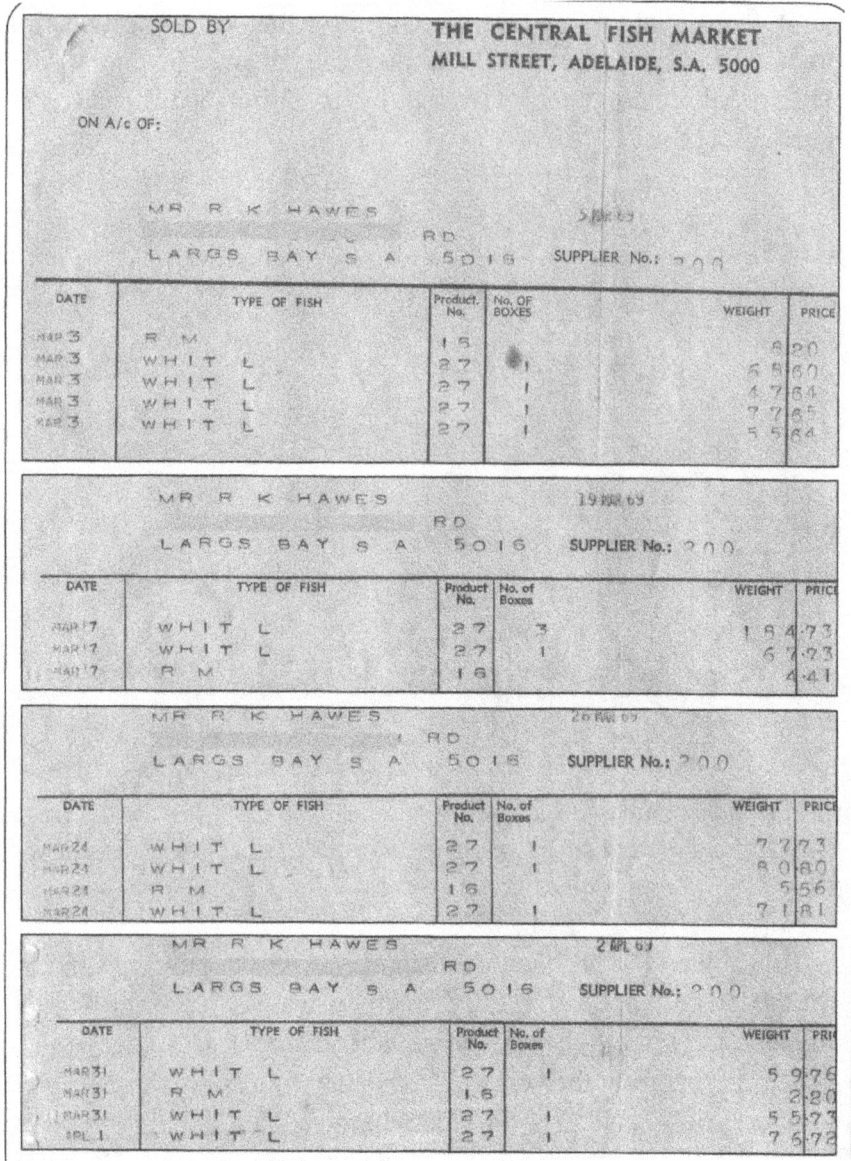

Our Central Fish Market receipts show that in March 1969 we caught, nine-hundred and sixty pounds of Whiting over four weekends. We would fish all day Saturday and half of Sunday.

On rough days, we knew a place where Whiting gathered not far from shore. We could fish there in safety, though getting there was not a comfortable journey. I recall two occasions when bad things happened. Both times I was on my own, and blinding spray was to blame. On the first occasion, I failed to notice how much spray had come into the boat until I changed course and almost swamped. The sudden lurch suggested I had a lot of water on board, and so I turned to inspect what was happening behind me. There was my quarter-empty fuel tank floating where water should not be. Carefully, I headed into the nearby beach, where I quickly began to bail. On the second occasion, I did not see a reef and ran the boat onto it. The boat slid completely out of the water. Luckily, no damage was done, but I had to wait for the tide to come in.

43 MICK ROONEY

Pop's job in the city brought him in contact with wide range of people. In the late fifties, Hemmingway and Robertson took on the Australian franchise for the Dale Carnegie Course. Dale Carnegie was the American author, well known for his iconic books, "How to Win Friends and Influence People" and "How to Stop Worrying and Start Living". The leadership course based on these books was well established in America, and quickly became essential training for many of Australia's top executives. The course ran for three months, with about 50 participants in each class.

Pop, with his experience in marketing and interest in psychology, was ideally suited to both sell the course, and conduct its sessions. Several hundred went through with Pop as the instructor, but one in particular drew his attention - Mick Rooney. Mick owned a signwriting business, which he had established upon returning from the war. Prior to the war, he and his two brothers had been commercial fishermen, living in Pine Point. That caught Pop's attention. The name Rooney often came up when locals talked about fishing in the old days. Lloyd Rooney was in fact still fishing at Pine Point, but Lloyd fished with nets, and we knew him only slightly.

Pop told Mick of his Pine Point fishing interests, which was something he told very few people. He was hoping that Mick could tell him interesting stories about the place, and he was right. However, the lecture room was not the place to have such a conversation. Arrangements were made for Mick to call in next time he visited back home.

It was a Friday night when Mick called in at Pine Point. Mum and I were introduced, and the TV was switched off. We all sat down to hear Mick's stories. First, he corrected a story Robbie had told years earlier. Robbie had been trying to frighten us from fishing the Harvester. He suggested that Port Lincoln Tom had taken Mick's brother, Colin. Mick told a very different story. Colin was 10 miles out at Long Spit on the day he disappeared. He was caught in an unexpected storm. I did not ask Mick if it was a westerly, though I strongly suspect it was.

Thanks to Mick, Robbie's credibility had taken yet another dive. Robbie's stories were always a combination of amazing facts together with some misleading whoppers. This was unfortunate, for I am sure most of the incredible things Robbie talked about, such as encounters with Killer Whales which he called Black Fish, were true.

Mick went on telling his stories, and to my surprise, he solved a mystery that had always puzzled me. He told a story I doubt many will believe, though we had no reason to doubt it. Our own experiences told us it was possible.

Moored in our little bay had been an 11-foot rowboat called Maria. It was an old boat and probably had a number of previous owners. Its owner, when I knew of it, was Clarrie Smallacombe, a rose nurseryman from Adelaide. Clarrie was the original owner of the shack visited by Pengwee, and he allowed me to use his boat whenever I wished. Often, I would row it around the bay checking shark lines that I had set. What puzzled me was the purpose for which the Maria was built. It was too small to have a motor, yet it had a well that could hold a good quantity of fish. I thought wells were for big boats that needed to keep their catch alive for several days at sea. The Maria could venture no further than rowing distance, and would have swamped in open water.

Mick described three boats that he and his brothers owned. They fitted the description of the Maria, though Mick did not recognise the name as being one of theirs. Each day, the brothers would row their boats a short distance out from Pine Point. There, they would use hand-lines to catch Whiting, which they kept alive in their wells. Nearby, they had a large floating cage on a mooring. At various times throughout the day, they would row to the cage and transfer their live catch into it. After several days, the cage would be full. Once full, they would tow the cage to shore and let it go dry on the tidal flat. Lastly, they would remove the fish and take them to the fish market.

I asked Mick how many fish it took to fill the cage. His answer, I have never forgotten. "Five hundred dozen," was his reply.

44 ROBBIE'S UNIMAGINABLE WHITING

As each season passed, we learned more about the habits of Whiting, and our catches grew. By 1969, Pop was selling his bigger catches to a fish buyer, as he believed putting too many Whiting through the fish market auction brought down his price.

Our minimum daily target by then was 10 dozen Whiting for the Pine Point grounds, and 20 dozen for the southern grounds. On Saturdays, we fished both grounds and the total target was 30 dozen. On Sundays, we only fished Pine Point, with its 10 dozen target. Often, we exceeded the target, but 30 dozen was a comfortable catch to handle. With Snapper, fish can be stacked to the top of the icebox. With Whiting, there is a risk of crushing once you go beyond a few layers of fish. Our Whiting always brought top price at Monday's market, and Pop did not want to sacrifice quality for quantity. We would store the Saturday catch overnight in the icebox, and the smaller Sunday catch went direct into fish market boxes.

Robbie had once made a pronouncement. He said there were more Whiting on the southern grounds than we could ever imagine. His advice had caused us to go there, and indeed, we had found an abundance of Whiting. However, Robbie was often cryptic with what he had to say, and something happened in 1969, about which I will always wonder.

Unfortunately, I could not ask Robbie, for Robbie and Rita were no longer with us. In 1967, Rita went into hospital for what I believe was a minor operation for an ingrown toenail. A few days later, she died suddenly while watching TV at Pine Point. Robbie said a blood clot was to blame. He was devastated. On the 3rd January, 1968, less than six months after losing Rita, a broken-hearted Robbie died from a heart attack in the Royal Adelaide Hospital. He was 63 years old.

It was in the year that followed Robbie's passing, that I witnessed an extraordinary event. The Whiting season was coming to an end and our regular drops on the southern grounds were almost devoid of fish. With nothing better to do, I decided to continue on our search pattern to see if I could find where the Whiting might have gone. I headed further out to sea, to a place I had looked several times before. The bottom there was part of the same reef system, but had fewer features than could be found closer to shore. Regardless, I decided to check it again.

The sea was calm that day, and I could see the bottom clearly. I arrived at the theoretical spot, expecting to see a rather uninspiring seabed. Instead, I came across a huge school of fish. The fish were within five feet of the surface and went almost to the bottom. They stretched in every direction for as far as I could see, and that was a good distance in calm water. They looked like Whiting but had to be small Salmon, for the school was one hundred times bigger than any Whiting school I had ever seen. I checked with my viewer. They were Whiting. Was this what Robbie meant when he promised more Whiting than we could ever imagine?

As I looked through the viewer, I noticed several squid hugging the sea floor. They were stalking the fish above. Squid are masters of camouflage, and I watched how easily they changed colour, continually matching what was beneath. I delayed fishing. I was curious about the squid. Suddenly, they rushed their prey and one grabbed a Whiting in a death grip. I did not realise that a squid could catch a Whiting, and wondered if these fish were asleep, or whatever it was fish did to rest.

I began fishing, without dropping ground bait, for ground bait seemed pointless under the circumstances. The fish were not asleep. They bit furiously, but my delight was short lived. I looked up and saw another boat about a mile away, headed directly at me. I quickly pulled anchor and moved away. If news got out about so many fish, an armada of boats would be drawn to the southern grounds in no time. Keeping Pop's drops secret was always foremost in my mind. The other boat stopped some distance away, but I still headed back to Pine Point, planning to return with Pop next day.

Next day we returned. The other boat was there again, anchored where it had stopped the day before. After a short deliberation, Pop decided that we should go to where I had found the fish, for he believed the fisherman in the other boat to be Bert Knapman.

Bert and his brother owned the two green sheds on the Black Point beach. The sheds had been there for much longer than we had been in the district. Occasionally, we would come across Bert out fishing. Pop believed he was now aged somewhere in his eighties.

Unfortunately, I never met the Knapman brothers, but I would have liked to. They would no doubt have had a wealth of stories to tell. It may well have been the Knapman brothers and not the Rooney brothers who found the Harvester ground. I know of no one who knows for certain. Stories become lost if not written down. Oddly enough, Bert Knapman lived only two streets behind us at Largs Bay. He was a boat builder, and we often heard the buzz of his circular saw when he was working on a boat.

We anchored up and I looked over the side with my viewer. The fish were still there. Fortunately, Bert's boat was too far away for him to see what we were doing, assuming that he did not bother with binoculars. Pop decided that we would remain seated and use hand-lines, making as few body movements as possible. Bert, or whoever it was in the other boat, would have no reason to think that we were catching a lot of fish. To minimise body movement further, the fish would be dropped on the floor, not put in the basket. Pop often adopted this plan when other boats were about.

Our actions for the next three hours were more mechanical than anything I can relate to fishing. Finally, we could not move in the boat without squashing fish. The floor was covered with Whiting, washing around in water we bucketed in to stop them drying out. Pop declared we had all we could handle and so we headed for home, leaving the other boat still anchored in the same place.

Back at the boat shed, we counted the fish as we iced them into fish boxes. We had forty-nine dozen and seven. I said to Pop that next time we should stay longer, to make sure we caught 50 dozen. But there never was a next time. That was the biggest catch of Whiting we ever had.

We returned to the spot the following weekend, but the fish were gone. We tried there the following season, but found few fish. That was the last year I fished with Pop as a commercial fisherman. I let my licence lapse. Fifteen years passed before I returned to that spot again. I journeyed there in 1985 and found several boats in the area. They were catching the odd Whiting, but there was no big school of fish. I never bothered to go back.

I have often wondered why the fish were gathered there that weekend. The gathering happened in April, which is their breeding month, but I think the fish were too small to breed. The size limit at the time was 11 inches, and many that we caught would not meet today's size limit of 12.2 inches (31 centimetres). Years later, I was invited by marine scientist Dr Tony Fowler, to be a part of an expedition on the fisheries research vessel, *Ngerin*. Tony was gathering data on spawning Whiting, and on one occasion, we fished a breeding school in deep water outside the gulf. Many of those fish displayed red blotches along their bellies and squirted milk when we brought them into the boat. I did not see anything like that with our big catch in 1969.

My guess is that the fish were getting ready to migrate to deeper water for the winter, and had all come to the one mustering point. The mustering point was close to the out-to-sea edge of the reef system, but what was more interesting to me, was that I found it by following our pattern of search.

45 A MORE NORMAL LIFE

In 1970, I took up a more normal life, as Frank had done 10 years earlier. Like Frank, I became an accountant and a family man, though fishing remaining a strong part of family living. I was lucky, for I married a very special girl.

Rosemary had never caught a fish before we met, but she quickly became an enthusiast. She joined me, as a member of Western Districts Angling Club, and was active in club events. After fishing a number of state championships, we became involved in the national championships that were held every two years. Along with son Paul and daughter Karyn, these championships took us to many parts of Australia. Rosemary was twice South Australia's State Lady Champion, before winning her first national title in 1999, and then repeating the effort in 2001. She also served for many years as both State and National Secretary for the Australian Anglers Association.

Rosemary is holding the Mr & Mrs Harold Watkins Trophy which is awarded by the Australian Anglers Association to the Overall State Champion Lady for the year. Rosemary won it twice. This photo was taken in 1987.

Sadly, Rosemary passed away in October 2013.

I managed one national title and a number of state titles. My main achievement was to have the honour of being appointed State Captain for nine national championship campaigns.

I am holding the City of Warrnambool Trophy that is awarded by the Australian Anglers Association to the Overall Champion State at a National Carnival. This photo was taken in 2001, shortly after South Australia won the trophy on Kangaroo Island.

Pop was also correct. I was never out of work as an accountant, but like with most jobs, much of what an accountant does can be both dull and repetitive. Fortunately, I found a niche in management accounting and made many good friends along the way. Had I chosen the life of a commercial fisherman, there would have been far fewer people in my life, and it is the people you have known and not the things you have done, that become your most precious memories.

Frank and I shared the same opinion on accountancy, and he did not remain an accountant for long; he joined the fledgling computer industry. During the seventies, while working for IBM, he was instrumental in the design and planning of IBM's first Australian Production Planning and Control System. The system ran on the IBM 360 model 20 mainframe, and later on the IBM 34 midrange computers. The Australian system proved so successful for production control and product costing, that it was subsequently adopted by many large manufacturers around the world, earning Frank an international reputation in the computer industry. Mrs Harvey would have been proud.

Pop retired from the world of commerce in 1966, at the age of 61. He had no superannuation and only modest savings. But the mortgage was paid, and Pop had no need for a retirement nest egg. His bank account was swimming in the sea, and he could make a withdrawal any time he wanted.

I was fortunate to have had Pop as my dad. His wisdom, humour, and attitude to life, are the things that will always make him my greatest hero. Pop was a tough taskmaster who seldom gave praise.

When I let my commercial fishing licence lapse in 1970, he was not happy. He saw my new interest in surf fishing as a waste of time.

Here, Trevor Hay is hosing the sand off Salmon we caught in the surf at "The Bottom End" of Yorke Peninsula.

In one season of surf fishing, I brought back seven ton of Salmon. Most went in the trailer, but sometimes I had to stack them in the back of the station wagon as well. Fortunately, recreational fishermen now have a ten fish bag limit, but at the time, we knew no better.

When I began fishing in competitions, he could see no point to it. When I became overall State Champion in 1971, he had nothing to say.

When Pop passed away in 1992, at the age of 86, Mum asked me to go through some of his things. I came across a small stack of newspapers gathering dust on top of his wardrobe. They were all from the one month, December 1971. There were multiple copies of two editions.

I thought Pop disapproved of my competition fishing, thinking it to be a waste of time. I was surprised, therefore, to find multiple copies of the same newspaper on top of his wardrobe after he passed away.

"Why did Pop have these?" I asked Mum.

Mum looked at the papers and recalled their importance. "Look through and you will find a story about you being State Champion," she replied.

I looked through and found one story in particular that had an impressive headline.

"I thought Pop disapproved of my club fishing," I commented.

Mum smiled. "He did, but he was proud when you won that, he just didn't want to tell you."

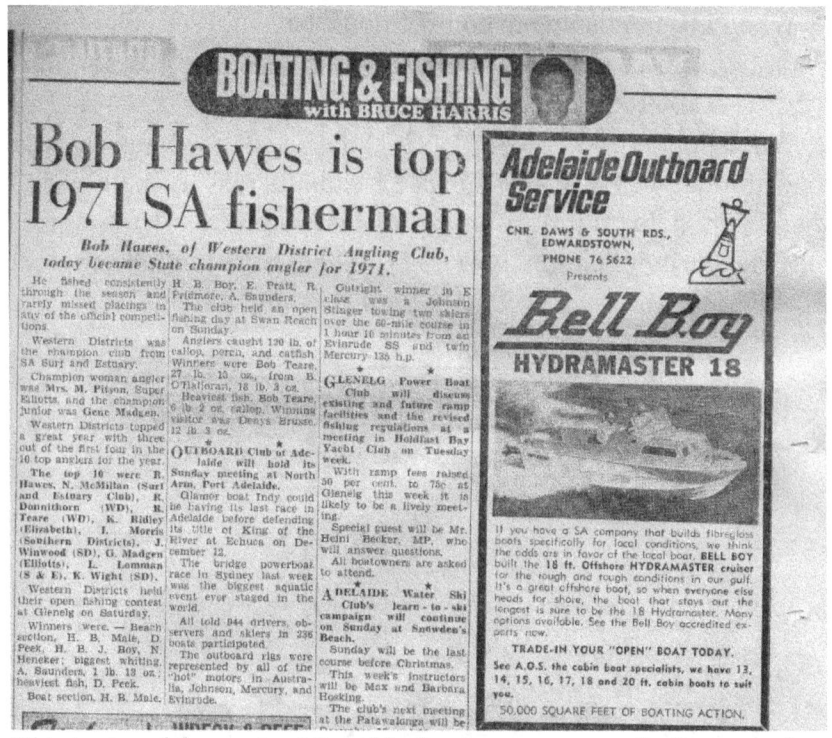

This is one of the stories I found in Pop's newspapers. In the years that followed, this type of publicity slowly disappeared from our general media, as conservationist and animal cruelty groups had begun to mount campaigns against recreational fishing. As a result, fishing club memberships declined. This was unfortunate, as fishing clubs are strong advocates for responsible angling.

Like Frank and his amazing result in the St Peters College IQ exam, I was only now learning things Pop was proud of at the time, but never told us.

Frank, Gwynne, and I, had all managed to make Pop proud, but Lloyd could not. His disability made it impossible. With no prospect of achieving anything of note, he had declared himself the black sheep of the family. He left home when 15 years old. For the next 20 years, he was a wanderer with no fixed address, only coming home when his legs were so ulcerated that only Mum could heal them. Then, in 1970, he had an extended stay at home, for his legs would not heal. That was when Pop and Lloyd finally got to know each other.

Apart from family and fishing, Pop's greatest interest was horseracing. He knew the performances of hundreds of racehorses, their jockeys, their trainers, and the tracks where they did best. His portable radio was never far from his side, as he constantly updated himself on all that was happening. The rest of us had no interest in the subject.

Then in 1970, Pop discovered for the first time that Lloyd shared his passion about racehorses. From then on, Lloyd and he were often in the lounge room, speculating on the winner of the next race to be broadcast on Pop's radio. In breaks between races, they would adjourn to the front room for a game of billiards. That year, Mum and Pop went to Queensland for a holiday. Lloyd went with them. Unfortunately, the new friendship lasted little more than a year. In September of 1971, we lost Lloyd in a car accident. We were all devastated, but somehow, I think Pop missed him the most.

Lloyd, Mum and Pop at the Currumbin Wildlife Sanctuary during their trip to Queensland. 1970.

A family snap shot. Pop, Karyn, Rosemary, Paul and Mum. Pop was not happy when I gave up commercial fishing, but the folks soon appreciated the additions to the family that resulted from my change in life style. 1979

46 MY RETURN TO PINE POINT

In 1985, I resumed fishing at Pine Point, this time as a recreational angler. I built a holiday house on Billy Goat Flat, close to Mum and Pop. I expected to find the fish where I left them, 15 years earlier. They were no longer there. Pop told me a sad story.

Shortly after I stopped fishing in 1970, the Government changed the law, and netting was permitted in water up to five metres deep at low tide. Prior to then, netting was banned seaward of the low water mark. The places where we caught most of our fish had all been netted out.

I began looking for Whiting in new places, and it was not long before I made a remarkable discovery. Pop no longer fished the Rock. He was 80 years old and his night fishing days were behind him. There was also no point, for the Snapper were no longer there. I decided to test the Rock for myself and discovered that the old fish magnet still existed. The place was alive with Whiting. The bag limit at the time was 30. I would go there with my fishing buddy, Colin Tanner, and we would be back by breakfast, with 60 Whiting.

Previously, we had caught very few Whiting at the Rock. I wondered if the fish that once inhabited the inshore reefs, somehow knew they had to move further out to avoid annihilation. However, the Rock was not a place Pop was happy for me to fish in daylight. There were now many boats around, and the Rock was his most secret ground. He asked me to find other places.

I guessed the bottom in the area of the Rock to be similar to that of the southern grounds, but the water was much deeper. I wondered if I could find new Whiting drops by using the pattern I had used in the sixties.

I had no sonar, and the big Trevally that had shown us the Rock, were all gone. However, Robbie's lessons helped again, and the persistent behaviour of a Dolphin suggested a location to begin. I found Whiting there. I now had two points from which to build the same pattern I had used on the southern grounds. The method appeared to work. Perhaps it was coincidence, perhaps not. Either way, in the two years that followed, I found seven excellent Whiting drops. All were in deep water and well away from the Rock.

That was 30 years ago. Since then, I have watched the fish in the area slowly decline. I would like to think that they have found new places, but where? They once thrived on the shallow reefs, but not anymore. The schools that visit such areas are now much smaller, and their stay is always brief. Sadly, I believe they struggle in their place of exile, and those magnificent schools will never be again.

The last 30 years have seen the 30 bag limit reduced to 12, and netting banned on the inshore reefs. Our marine scientists maintain a vigilant watch. They know what fish we have, but do not know what we once had. I believe scientific collection of comprehensive catch and effort data only began in 1983, well after the netting of the inshore reefs had begun. The records show the trend, but not the total decline, which probably began shortly after World War II.

In 1952, the year Pop and Frank first entered the Black Point bay aboard the *Teal*, the beach was lined by thick scrub. There were no boats out fishing. That same beach is now prime real estate, where more than 100 prestigious holiday homes face the water. Locals call it Millionaires Row. People treasure the place and enjoy the fishing. I hope that future generations will continue to enjoy the fishing, but the trend is worrisome.

47 ROBBIE'S RIDDLE

Over the years, Pop and I worked out many of the complex rules that Whiting appeared to follow. It was Pop's intellectual property, acquired for the purpose of finding fish and catching them. The weather, the tide, the season, and the terrain of the sea floor, all played a part. When Pop and I fished for Whiting, it was like going to the hen house and collecting the eggs. The rules told us when and where the fish would be. When Mum went with us to the southern grounds, she always asked to be at the Big Hole just before the turn of tide. She would look over the side, waiting for the fish to arrive. On cue, they would stream into the hole. "Here come my little soldiers marching in a line," she would say. Then we would fish. It was her ritual. The Whiting knew where they had to be and were always there on time. The water could be cloudy or clear, it made no difference. The fish did not have to see to know where they were going.

Robbie once gave me some cryptic advice. He suggested that the reason why fish are never lost was a puzzle we had to solve. I often wondered how close we came to solving his puzzle. There are many theories on the subject. We concluded that Whiting used all their senses when finding their way around, but the sense of smell is paramount, and the most important smell is that of other Whiting.

Often, I would use my glass bottom viewer to watch what Whiting did at the turn of the tide. At first, the water would be slack, and I would see no fish. Then everything changed as the current began to flow. Whiting would appear out of nowhere and begin to feed on the reef. Feeding would last for about 20 minutes, and then fish would start to gather in a school about five feet from the bottom. The school would build in numbers as more fish gave up feeding.

The school would be up tide, where it patrolled the width of the reef, always swimming at right angles to the current. We guessed they were laying a scent trail in the water, which the feeding fish could smell and know the location of the school. We incorporated this probability into our search pattern for Whiting. We assumed that Whiting used scent to fix the locations of their schooling places. These schooling places were in turn located within fixed zones, outside of which we would find few Whiting. A minimum of two scent trails marked a zone, as the tide reverses direction every six hours. During the day, Whiting schools travelled between zones, but did not linger long as they had to keep their scent trails within the zones.

This aspect of the theory was the only way we could explain why Whiting avoided so much of the good feeding bottom on the southern grounds. When I used the theory to find Whiting off Pine Point, I discovered that Ron Harvey's Rock had few Whiting. This supported the theory, as Ron's drop appeared to lay between two zones. The theory also explained why fish are less active during periods of a dodge tide. Water needs to be moving in order to carry scent.

I think Robbie also gave a cryptic clue. On the day he set his riddle, he told me that he followed the reefs and they were easy to follow, because the reefs in the gulf all ran in the same direction. This was information I later discarded as one of his misleading whoppers, because I found reefs that ran in all directions. However, I now believe Robbie was telling a half-truth. My guess is that he followed scent trails when looking for fish.

There is a lot more that could be said about the zones, their sizes, the distances between them, and how they fitted into our search pattern, but all that matters in this story is - I believe scent was the key to solving Robbie's riddle.

As a final word, when netting commenced on the inners reefs, which was the Whiting's preferred territory, the fish migrated further out-to-sea. I think the sudden decline of inshore fish caused a corresponding reduction in the strength of the scent that marked their inshore zones. As a result, they were attracted to zones further out, where their scent was now comparatively stronger. These outer zones had always existed, but previously carried a much smaller population. That is how Pop's Rock and other places, suddenly gained Whiting in far greater numbers than before.

Unfortunately, all this was just our theory. It was what we thought we could see happening. It gave us the method we used when looking for Whiting. Had marine scientists studied what we first found, they may have proved a key part of one of nature's great mysteries – *Why Fish Never Get Lost*. King George Whiting was the perfect species to study. Gulf St. Vincent, with its modest depth of water and dodge tide every fortnight, the perfect laboratory.

The laboratory is still there, but the lab rats have all gone. We can no longer observe them in shallow water, and the few that survive no longer live the old way. They live a nomadic existence, hunted from place to place. Here one day, gone the next. If our theory has substance, then the structure that once guided them through their world is in shambles. They no longer have the numbers needed to define their territory with scent, and they struggle to survive in their place of exile. The behaviour we once saw can no longer be observed.

The people of Adelaide never realised that they had a marine jewel on their doorstep, and those of us who found it, never understood it. We thought it was robust, and would be there forever. We were wrong. Now we can only tell of how it was, in that time not so long ago - when Pop took us fishing.

ABOUT THE AUTHOR

Bob Hawes' life has revolved around fishing since the age of three. This book describes his early exploits with his father, which began in 1948. In later years, Bob became involved with the Australian Anglers Association at both a State and Federal level. He captained the South Australian Team on nine occasions, and won a number of individual State and a National Title.

www.ingramcontent.com/pod-product-compliance
Lightning Source LLC
Chambersburg PA
CBHW070427010526
44118CB00014B/1942